Zacharias Tanee Fomum

The Art of Working Hard

Éditions du Livre Chrétien
4, rue du Révérend Père Cloarec
92400 Courbevoie France
editionlivrechretien@gmail.com

Published by

EDITIONS DU LIVRE CHRÉTIEN

4, rue du Révérend Père Cloarec

92400 Courbevoie - FRANCE

Tél : (33) 9 52 29 27 72

Email : editionlivrechretien@gmail.com

I LOVINGLY DEDICATE THIS BOOK TO

EMILIA NDINTEH

A WOMAN OF GOD INVOLVED IN THE BATTLE

TO CONQUER PLANET EARTH

FOR OUR LORD JESUS CHRIST.

Preface

Preface

All the people who have made impact on history varied in many things, but they all had one thing in common - they worked hard. It is only true that "The heights by which great men reached and kept were not attained by sudden flight but while their companions slept, they kept toiling upwards into the sky."

The Lord has given us work to do. He desires it accomplished. If we are to accomplish that work, we must put all that we are and all that we have into it. As far as this book is concerned, we must work with all our might. Only then can we satisfy His heart.

This book is written on working hard. We acknowledge that there are other important things in the whole matter of satisfying the heart of God. In this book, we have tried to concentrate on working hard. The other aspects of satisfying God's heart have been covered or will be covered in our other books.

- You can work hard and satisfy the heart of God.
- You can work hard and win an eternal reward.
- You can work hard in preparation for a high rank in the Kingdom of God.

- You can work hard and improve your position on earth spiritually.
- You can work hard and improve your situation on earth in all ways.
- What you can do, you should do.
- What you should do, you must do.
- What you must do, you must do it with all your might.
- What you must do with all your might, you should do at once.
- The Lord God worked hard and works hard.
- The Lord Jesus worked hard and works hard.
- The Holy Spirit is working hard.
- You go and do likewise.

We have written a companion volume to this book entitled, "Deliverance from the Sin of Laziness." Those who are lazy should read that book first and be delivered from laziness, and then, as they become free, they should read this one and master the art of working hard.

We write the book, not from a position of people who have "arrived", but as people who are at work, mastering and applying the principles that are written here.

If you have been blessed by this book and been enabled to make more progress in working hard, please let us know and may the Lord bless you abundantly.

This book is the ninth in the series: "PRACTICAL HELPS FOR OVERCOMERS." The books in that series include the following:

Book 01 : The Use of Time

Book 02 : Retreats for Spiritual Progress

Book 03 : Personal Spiritual Revival

Book 04 : Daily Dynamic Encounters with God

Book 05 : The School of Truth

Book 06 : How to Succeed in the Christian Life

Book 07 : The Christian and money

Book 08 : Deliverance from the Sin of Laziness

Book 09 : **The Art of Working Hard.**

13th September 1988.

Zacharias Tanee Fomum,

P.O. BOX 6090,

YAOUNDE - CAMEROON.

PREPARING TO WORK HARD

1

The indispensability of a goal.

It is extremely difficult to work hard without a goal in view. No one can work hard for the sake of working hard. Finally, each person who has decided to work hard must decide on the goal that he has in mind for working hard.

The Lord Jesus worked hard. He had a clear goal in mind. He said, "*My food is to do the will of him who sent me, and to accomplish his work . Do you not say, 'There are yet four months, then comes the harvest'? I tell you, lift up your eyes, and see how the fields are already white for harvest. He who reaps receives wages, and gathers fruit for eternal life, so that the sower and reaper may rejoice together.*" (John 4:34-36). He again said,"*And I have other sheep, that are not of this fold; I must bring them also, and they will heed my voice. So there shall be one flock, one shepherd.*" (John 10:16). Furthermore, He said, "*We must work the works of him who sent me, while it is day; night comes, when no one can work.*" (John 9:4).

Having therefore a clear goal which was to give Himself as a ransom for many, and small goals that would lead to the major goal being accomplished, the Lord laboured on purposefully. He put in all of Himself at each moment with a clear goal in view, and that goal was contributory to His master goal. For example, when He talked with the Samaritan woman at the well of Jacob, He was not carrying out a conversation to keep things going while waiting for His food to come. He was labouring for her salvation and that of others. Because He had a clear goal, He gave Himself totally to it. Although He was weary, tired and hungry, He did not allow any of these to deter Him. He put weariness, tiredness and hunger aside and laboured to win her into the kingdom. So preoccupied was He with ministering to her that when food came, He did not give Himself to it but rather said, "*I have food to eat of which you do not know,*" (John 4:32), and "*My food is to do the will of him who sent me, and to accomplish his work.*" (John 4:34). It would have been impossible for the Lord to exert Himself so completely and so totally if there had been no goal in view.

The apostle Paul worked hard. He was goal-directed. He said, "*I am under obligation both to the Greeks and to barbarians, both to the wise and to the foolish: so I am eager to preach the gospel to you also who are in Rome.*" (Romans 1:14-15). He again said, "*For necessity is laid upon me. Woe is me if I do not preach the gospel.*" (1 Corinthians 9:16). Also, "*I try to please all men in every thing I do, not seeking my own advantage, but that of many, that they may be saved.*" (1 Corinthians 10:33). "*Every athlete exercises self control in all things. They do it to receive a perishable wreath, but we an imperishable. Well, I do not run aimlessly, I do not box as one beating the air.*" (1 Corinthians 9:25-26). He also said, "*One thing I do, forgetting what lies behind and straining forward to what lies ahead, I press on toward the goal for the prize of the upward call of God in Christ Jesus.*" (Philippians 3:13-14). He had a clear goal . He had a master goal and smaller goals to help him to accomplish the master goal.

There must be a master passion, a supreme goal, a great burden on a man's heart without which he cannot work hard all the time. This passion, goal, or burden, must be clear and it must be deeply embedded in a person. It must be such that it can push the person to labour on and on unsupervised. There are some people who will work hard under supervision . They are forced from outside to work hard. They have a goal in thus working hard to please the person who is looking. That will last for as long as the person is watching. However, it is not that type of working hard that we have in mind. We are thinking about the working hard that has become a way of life; something that flows from inside. We are thinking about a life-principle that has become an integral part of a person's being so that even if he were shut somewhere alone with no one to see him, he would still give himself to hard work. Let us look at the matter of a master goal and the small goals that will help it to be accomplished. Let us take the example of someone who wants to become the leader of a big company. His master goal is to become the leader of that company. How will he go about accomplishing this master goal ? To do that, he must establish smaller goals which when accomplished, will enable the master goal to be accomplished. These may include:

1. Working hard at doing his present job excellently. This will involve:
2. Putting extra time into study.
3. Putting extra working hours into the work,
- coming earlier than others.
- going away later than others.
4. Labouring to take away any physical handicaps that may be in the way. For example, if the person has overweight and sees this as a possible obstacle, he will set a goal on cutting down his weight.
5. Etc.

6. Building the right relationships with his superiors and inferiors.
7. Etc.

He will set goals in each of these areas, and as he accomplishes them, he will be moving nearer his master goal. When, say, a superior or an inferior is rude to him, he will not react just as he feels. He will ask, "How can I react in this situation in such a way that it will help me to one day become the boss of this company ?" By asking that question, he will certainly not respond according to how hurt he is but according to its impact on the future. If there is more work to do, he will not complain about the extra time involved, but will decide to work hard to build the company that he will one day direct.

Applying it to other examples in the christian life, let us look at the person who wants to become an elder in a local assembly. His master goal is to become an elder. He will work hard at the following:

1. Studying the qualifications that the Bible gives for one who aspires to that office. He will do this diligently.
2. He will honestly analyze himself to see where he falls short.
3. He will own up that he falls short in these areas.
4. He will work out a strategy to put on that which is lacking.
5. He will not rest until it is done.
6. He will develop the right attitude towards those leading him and those below him.

We recommend that this person should settle the following very clearly.

1. What is the goal of my life ? The goal should be stated clearly in one sentence.
2. How long will it take to accomplish that goal ?
3. Will I be totally fulfilled when that goal is accomplished ?
4. Have I broken the master goal into smaller goals which when put together will enable the overall goal to be accomplished ?
5. Do I have a goal for the next five years?
6. Is the goal such that, when it would have been accomplished, will contribute to the accomplishment of my master (life's) goal?
7. Do I have a goal for this year?
8. How is this year's goal related to the five years' goal and to the master goal?
9. Do I have a goal for this month?
10. How is it related to the year's goal?
11. Do I have a goal for this week?
12. How is it related to this month's goal?
13. How is it related to the master goal?
14. Do I have a goal for this day?
15. How is it related to the week's, month's, year's, five years and master goal?
16. Do I have a goal for this hour?
17. How is it related to the goal of the day and the overall goal?

Any life without a master goal is a wasted life. Any year without clear goals having been set to be accomplished in it is a wasted year, and all without goals will become lazy. Any day or hour without any goal planned to be accomplished in it, is a wasted day and wasted hour, and those who produce wasted hours are not hard-working.

18. Have you a clear goal for the

    year

    month

    week

    day

    hour

    that is before you? Are the goals written down? If not, do something about it now! Do not waste the year, month, week, day, hour.

19. Is the goal you have for your life the one that when accomplished, will make the greatest impact for the Lord Jesus on planet earth?

20. Is the goal that you have established for the next five years

    year

    month

    week

    day

    hour

    the best to help you to accomplish that life's goal ?

2

The size of your goal

When you settle on the goal that you have set for your life, you should make sure that the goal is big enough to demand your all. You should make sure that the goal is big enough to be worthy of you.

In order to have that which is worthy of you, you need to see yourself in a true perspective. Who do you think knows you the best ?

Is it yourself ?

Is it your parents ?

Is it your friend ?

Although you know yourself to some extent and although your parents or your friend may know you better than yourself, there is One who knows you as indeed you are. His knowledge of you is not based on guesses or presumptions. It is based on truth. That person is the Lord God. He knows you because He made you. He knows you further because He redeemed you. His knowledge of you is perfect. What He says you are is the absolute truth. The question is, "What does He say you are?"

God says you are a God

God says of you in His word, the Bible, *I say, "You are gods, sons of the Most High, all of you."* (Psalm 82:6).His word again says, "*God has taken his place in the divine council in the midst of the gods he holds judgment.*" (Psalm 82:1).

The Lord Jesus confirmed this by saying, "*Is it not written in your law, I said, you are gods'? If he called them gods to whom the word of God came (and scripture cannot be broken), do you say of him whom the Father consecrated and sent into the world, 'You are blaspheming,' because I said, I am the Son of God ?*" (John 10:34-36)

If God says that you are a god, you must be a god. If you believe that you are less than a god, contradict God and thereby attempt to make Him a liar. We know that He cannot lie. You must be a god and you ought to yield to His word about you and own up to the fact that you are a god.

I want you to confess aloud that you are a god. Say aloud, I,...X...., am a god. God who made me and redeemed me says that I am a god. He knows best what He made and what He redeemed. He must be correct. I am a god ! I am a god! I am a god!!

What God made you into

The Bible says concerning you, "*When I look at the heavens, the works of thy fingers, the moon and the stars which thou hast established; what is man that thou art mindful of him, and the son of man that thou dost care for him? Yet thou hast made him little less than God, and dost crown him with glory and honour. Thou hast crowned him with glory and honour. Thou hast given him dominion over the works of thy hands; thou hast put all things under his feet, all sheep and oxen, and also the beasts of the field, the birds of the air, and the fish of the sea, whatever passes along the paths of the sea."* (Psalm 8:3-8).

God has made you little less than Himself! What a statement! The God who created the entire universe, the God who sustains it, the all-knowing, all-wise and all-powerful God says that He made you a little less than Himself. It means that He made you almost

all-knowing,

all-wise and

all-powerful !

Do you believe that ? If you believe it, you will function fully as He meant you to function. If you do not believe it, you will not rise up to what you are meant to be; to what indeed you are.

You are not what you think you are.

You are not what people say you are.

You are not what you have proved to be.

You are not what you have tried to be.

YOU ARE WHAT GOD SAYS YOU ARE. YOU ARE JUST THAT.

WHAT GOD HAS GIVEN YOU

In the beginning, before God created man, He said, "*Let us make man in our image, after our likeness; and let them have dominion over the fish of the sea, and over the birds of the air, and over the cattle, and over all the earth, and over every creeping thing that creeps upon the earth. So God created man in his own image, in the image of God he created him; male and female he created them. And God blessed them, and God said to them, be fruitful and multiply, and fill the earth and subdue it; and have dominion over the fish of the sea, and over the birds of the air, and over every living thing that moves upon the earth.*" (Genesis 1:26-28).

God created man in His likeness. God created man to have dominion over the fish of the sea,

the birds of the air,

the cattle,

all the earth,

every creeping thing.

God commanded the man He created to have dominion over

the fish of the sea,

the birds of the air,

every living thing.

That was what He intended and did at the beginning. Even after the fall of man and with the redemption in mind, God did not change His mind. Man remained a little less than God and God still crowned him with glory and honour. God still gave him dominion over the works of His hands and put all things under his feet :

- all the sheep and oxen,
- all the beasts of the field,
- all the birds of the air,
- all the fish of the sea,
- all that passes along the path of the sea. (Psalm 8:4-8).

After the redemption was achieved, God continued to reaffirm, and the reaffirmation is even more valid, "*Thou hast crowned him with glory and honour, putting everything in subjection under his feet. Now, in putting everything in subjection to him, he left nothing outside his control.*" (Hebrews 2:7-8).

God has given you authority to function as your very self; that is, as a god. God has put everything in subjection under your feet!

- God has crowned you with honour and glory!
- God has left nothing outside your control!
- God has given you dominion over all the works of His hands!
- God has given you everything that it takes to be a god, a little less than Himself!

The size of your goal

Because you are what God has made you to be; because you are what God says you are; you are to make a goal for yourself that is God-sized. You are to make a goal for yourself which when accomplished, will give God an opportunity to say, "This one is my product. He acts almost like Me!"

His exhortation to you is, "*Ask of me and I will make the nations your heritage, and the ends of the earth your possession.*" (Psalm 2:8).

If you accept that you are what God says you are, you will not settle for anything less. Mario Murillo said, "You are a child of God. That means that, to do anything below what you were created to do, will bore you. Your supernatural origin and the legacy of triumph that makes up the Christian faith demand that you do something about your life."

If you think that you are a failure or that you are not of much consequence, you will fall short of your potential.

When the twelve spies returned from spying the land of canaan, ten of them said, "*We are not able to go up against the people; for they are stronger than we... The land through which we have gone, to spy it out, is a land that devours its inhabitants; and all the people that we saw in it are men of great stature. And there we saw the Nephilim (the sons of Anak, who come from the Nephilim) and we seemed to ourselves like grasshoppers and so we seemed to them.*" (Numbers 13:31-33).

These people saw themselves as grasshoppers. They could not do what God-ordained people could do. They confessed their inability. They refused God's confession that they were able to possess the land. Because they confessed something else apart from what the Lord said, they became what they confessed instead of what God had made them into, and perished in the wilderness. Two of them, Joshua and Caleb confessed what God said about them and God stood with them and made it true in them, and for them. They therefore entered the Promised Land and possessed it.

What you believe about yourself will affect your goal.

The size of your goal will determine whether or not you will become a hard-working person.

People who have great goals and are determined to accomplish them become people who work very hard; for very hard work is indispensable for the accomplishment of any great goal.

You are a god.

Set a God-sized goal for yourself.

You are a little less than God.

Set a goal for yourself that is a little less than that which God has set for Himself.

You are the son of the King. Set goals that befit the King and the Kingdom. You are working for the King. Do work for Him that befits His glory, majesty and power.

Do not say that you are not able. "Confess with the apostle, *I can do all things in him who strengthens me*." (Philippians 4:13).

Do not give up because of your weaknesses; for His power is made perfect in weakness.

I command you to arise and dream great things for your God.

I command you to arise and set a great goal for your God.

I command you to arise and accomplish your great goal and thereby accomplish great things for your God.

Do not concentrate on your limitations. David had only five small stones and he accomplished his great goal of that day. He killed the well-armed Goliath. You are able! You are able!! You are able!!!

3

The indispensability of training.

The person who wants to accomplish his goal in the shortest possible time and as efficiently as possible, needs to be trained. Training enables the person to work hard.

Let me take a situation from working on a farm. When someone goes to work on a farm for the first time, he may cut grass in a limited area for six hours and get home with a lot of blisters that will make it impossible for him to return to work on the farm for a number of days until his blisters have healed. However, an experienced farmer may clear as much as ten times the area cleared by the inexperienced one in the same length of time and have no blisters. He will thus be able to go to the farm everyday.

Each one must learn to work hard. No one is born naturally hard-working. The personality has to be trained and disciplined to work hard. The best training is the one that is imparted gradually in the course of life.

The best thing is that a child ought to have been trained to work hard. The Bible says, "***Train up a child in the way he should go, and when he is old he will not depart from it.***" (Proverbs

22:6). Hard-working parents will normally train their children to work hard, simply by providing hard-working models for the children. Personally, I never learned to work hard as a conscious process. I was blessed to have been born to a father and mother who worked hard.

However, whether or not a person learned to work hard in childhood, it does not ultimately matter. The person who is determined to accomplish his goal will teach himself how to work hard. If he is desperate enough to accomplish his goal, he will pay any price that is necessary. He will labour at removing any obstacles that stand on his way at any cost. This requires discipline. Training to work hard is more or less training in discipline.

Discipline is the purposeful putting of oneself under control in order to achieve a desired result. The one who is going to accomplish a great goal will put himself under discipline. What does this mean in practice? It means that for a person who is studying, when the work that has been set apart for the day has not been accomplished and there is a feeling of sleepiness, he will not yield to sleep. Rather, he will walk round the room, go outside for a walk or a run or do any other thing to drive away sleep. When that has been done, he will return to work and keep at it until the work is accomplished. He has thereby begun to train his body to say "No" to sleep. If he continues that way, he can reduce his sleeping time from eight hours a night to seven hours a night and then to six hours a night and then to five hours a night and then to four hours a night. He will correspondingly be increasing his working time from say twelve hours a day to thirteen hours a day, to fourteen hours a day, to fifteen hours a day, to sixteen hours a day.

We say from hard-earned experience, that the body is not an enemy but a servant to be trained. The body can be trained to need eight hours of sleep a night in order to function efficiently or to function efficiently on four hours or even two hours of sleep a night. I once read of a Head of State of a certain country who was called a "workaholic." This man had disciplined himself to functioning efficiently on two hours of sleep per night and he had lived that way for all the five years since he became president.

Maybe the following story will communicate to you what we are labouring to say. "*God disciplines us for good, that we may share His holiness.*" (Hebrews 12:10). When they are received aright, the disciplines of life serve to produce in us the likeness of Christ. I saw this exhibited to a remarkable degree in the life of one of God's choicest hidden saints. My visit to the home of Miss H.R.Higgen in Melbourne will not soon be forgotten.

She had neither arms nor legs, for these had been progressively amputated to arrest a bone disease. She named her cottage 'Gladwish', and for forty-three years never left her room. When I entered, it was not to see a depressed invalid, but a radiant christian. Instead of bemoaning the hardness of her lot, she gave herself to prayer and spiritual ministry.

To the end of the stump of one arm, a fountain pen was fastened, while on the other stump there was a rubber attachment. With these, she managed to manipulate a stand and letter rack by her bedside. When the calamity overtook her, instead of rebelling against God, she took it from Him as a discipline intended to accelerate the formation of Christ in her.

She mastered the difficult art of writing and developed an almost copper-plate style. Then began a correspondence that circled the globe. People from all over the world visited that little room, and no one left without being impressed by the triumph of Christ which she demonstrated.

Her help showed me letters from people the world around whom she had led to Christ, either in that little room or through her correspondence. Literally, hundreds were brought to Christ through her radiant testimony. The circumstances which might well have crushed and embittered her, only served to sweeten and make her more like her Master. She exemplified Catherine Booth Clibborn's hymn:

Turn your trouble into treasure,

Turn your sorrow into song,

Then the world will know the measure

In which you to Christ belong.

(Osward Smith in "This I remember")

The apostle Paul wrote, "*Every athlete exercises self-control in all things. They do this to receive a perishable wreath, but we an imperishable. Well, I do not run aimlessly, I do not box as one beating the air; but I pommel my body and subdue it, lest after preaching to others I myself should be disqualified.*" (I Corinthians 9:25-27).

We repeat that the body is a servant that is wild and needs to be tamed to serve properly. Take the area of food. It is quite interesting to know that eating much food and working hard at praying are mutually exclusive. The person who has decided to work hard in the school of prayer will discipline himself to eat only the minimum amount of food that will allow him to function properly. We know that there are people who eat three or four times the quantity of food that other people of the same height eat. It is not that some bodies need more food than others, but that some bodies have been trained to need more food than others.

In the training to work hard, no one can run away from enduring. The one who grows in discipline also grows in endurance. There will be many calls to give up, but the one who endures keeps going. There will be many obstacles, but the one who has trained himself to overcome, keeps pressing on and keeps forcing one obstacle after the other to give way. He is determined that no obstacle will keep him away from accomplishing the goal before him. When faced with an obstacle, he does not ask, "Will this be removed ?" Instead he asks, "Which is the quickest way to remove this obstacle?" To him, the obstacle must be removed at any cost. The only question is how it should be removed. If it takes ten days to remove the obstacle, he will labour for ten days. If it requires ten weeks, he will labour for ten weeks. One thing is sure; the obstacle must be removed and he labours at it until it is removed.

The one who wants to work hard will also train himself to think correctly. He knows the power of thoughts. He will divorce himself permanently from any thoughts that suggest that there is pleasure in being at ease and being idle. He will shut himself away from thoughts that suggest rest while the work is not completed and some energy is left. He will fill himself with the thoughts of the God who works hard and the reward that He has reserved for them who work hard. The Bible says, "*It is the hard-working farmer who ought to have the first share of the crops*." (Timothy 2:6). "*If we endure we shall also reign with him*." (Timothy 2:12).

So the person who wants to really work hard will discipline all of his body.

4

Investing everything into the goal

By the help of the Lord, you have accepted what God says you are and you believe Him absolutely. You believe Him so completely that there is an inward song in your heart which says,

"I am a god.

I am God's child.

I am the King's son.

I must act like myself

I must do great things for the King."

Someone is suggesting that you are a failure. Your answer to him is,

"I cannot be a failure

I am God's success.

I was created for dominion.

I have been given dominion.

I have a great goal.

I will exercise dominion.

I will exercise dominion by accomplishing the great goal.

I will not fail because God lives in me.

God is at work in me.

God is at work with me and He cannot fail."

Because God cannot fail, I cannot fail.

A SUPREME GOAL NEEDS ALL OF YOU

you have the one goal of your life. That goal when accomplished will bring the greatest glory to God that can come from you. A supreme goal can only be accomplished at supreme cost. A supreme goal can only be accomplished by investing every thing that you are and that you have into accomplishing it.

If you hold back anything from your goal, you have decided to fail. Because you do not want to fail, you must decide that you will let your goal have all that you are and all that you have.

God had a great goal. It was to redeem man. The goal was so big, so supreme that He gave it all that He had. The Lord Jesus is God's all, and God gave Jesus Christ in order to accomplish His goal. When He gave Jesus Christ, He had nothing left but Himself, and He also gave Himself in order to accomplish His goal, for the Bible says, "*God was in Christ reconciling the world to Himself.*" (II Corinthians 5:9).

Since our theme is hard work, we shall look at other things that must be invested into the accomplishment of your goal in passing and then dwell on that which has to do with hard work. We have said that a supreme goal demands your all. This will include:

1. All your physical power,
2. All your will power,
3. All your mental power,
4. All your emotional power,
5. All your money,
6. All your time,
7. Everything else.

In order to succeed, you will put in all these and be undisturbed by the cost. You will be so wrapped up with your goal that you will not bother about what it is costing you. Others may say that you are sacrificing, but the sacrifice will be a joy to you because of the joy of having your goal accomplished. Any pain caused will be endured because of the expected reward. The Bible says of the Lord Jesus that *For the joy that was set before Him endured the Cross, despising the shame, and is seated at the right hand of the throne of God.* (Hebrews 12:12).

To accomplish your goal, you have to work very, very hard. You have to put in all the energy that you can possibly put in. You have to put in all the energy that you can possibly put in and in the most intelligent way possible. You have to put in all the energy that you can possibly put in for the longest possible time. You have to hold nothing back.

In investing your energy, you have to ensure that you invest it wisely. It will have to be invested in such a way that the goal is accomplished in the shortest possible time. It will have to be invested in such a way that you are not destroyed before the goal is accomplished. One thing you will do throughout is to ensure that you are not holding back any ounce of energy that you could put into working to accomplish the goal. You will have to ensure that nothing is done in two days that could be done in one day.

The goal that God sets for a person to accomplish in his life is such that it needs the person putting in all of himself and all that he has for all of his life in order to accomplish it. Any loss of time is crippling to the entire goal. Therefore, the person who wants to succeed has no time to waste and no time to be careless with. Every minute counts.

5

The critical importance of time.

One of the greatest gifts that God has given to mankind is time. In the distribution of time, God has no favourites. He has given to each person the same number of hours per day - twenty four. The Head of State and the beggar, each has twenty four hours as a free gift from God.

One thing that distinguishes great men from failures is how this great gift called time is invested by them. All those who invest time wisely succeed. All those who invest time foolishly fail. A successful person is one who has learnt to invest time properly. The successful person spends time with greater economy than he would spend money. He realizes that although time is a free gift from God, it is a most perishable gift. Once lost, it is most likely lost forever.

The person who will succeed will invest his time in accomplishing his goal. He will have no time for anything else. He is of necessity narrow. He cuts away all the neutral

good

better and

best things.

He gives himself to only one thing - the must of his life. The must of his life is what must be done to accomplish his goal in the shortest possible time.

If you are reading this message at the age of, say, twenty-five, and if we take for granted that you will live actively until you are seventy, we know for certain that you have forty-five years to go. Forty-five years may look like a long time, but it is not. How have you spent the last twenty-five years ? How fruitfully have you invested them ? How far have you gone in the accomplishment of your life's goal ? Could it be that at twenty-five you do not yet have a master goal for your life ? This would mean that you have only forty-five years to find out what the goal of your life is and accomplish it before your time is up.

Let us look at the issue more closely. You possibly spend six hours sleeping at night and one hour having siesta in the day. In addition, you possibly spend one hour bathing, dressing and cleaning up. Then, you possibly spend two hours preparing food, serving it and tidying the place in addition to shopping and all that goes with feeding yourself. Your friends, visitors, wife (husband), children and all the rest of humanity, may consume an average of another three hours a day. Possibly, another hour is taken up by unforeseen circumstances. We can write this out as follows :

1.

1. Sleep	07 hours
2. Personal hygiene	01 hour
3. Eating	02 hours
4. Relationships	03 hours
5. Unforeseen	01 hour
	---------------
	14 hours

This means that if you diligently use the rest of your time, you have only 10 hours left to accomplish the goal of your life.

This means that if you are twenty-five years old today, you have 10/24 x 45 years= 18.9 years actually available to accomplish your life's goal.

This means that if you are 30 years today, you have 10/24 x 40 = 16.7 years available.

If you are 40 years today, you have only 10/24 x 30/1 = 12.5 years available.

If you are 50 years today, you have only 10/24 x 20/1 = 8.3 years available.

Do you see that regardless of how young you may be, you do not have much time available ? Do you see that if you are already 40 or 50 years old, then your time is short, very short ?

You will realize that of the 10 hours that are available, if you work for 8 hours a day at earning your living, and you work five days a week, you do spend about one hour on going to work plus 8 hours at work.

This means that you have 8 x 5 = 40 hours

5 x 1 = 5 hours

----

45 hours

The forty-five hours average to 45 divided by 7 = 6.4 hours. This means that you will indeed have only 10.0 - 6.4 hours = 3.6 hours in which to know the Lord deeply and accomplish His call on your life.

This makes the matter of time even more important since without time being available, you cannot accomplish the goal of your life.

My fear is that there are people who spend less than two hours a day doing the most important job on Planet Earth which is to know God and serve Him in preparation for rulership in the world to come. Could anything be worse than this ?

Consider the magnitude of eternity. Let us take for example that eternity shall be one hundred trillion years. This means that God has given each one of us 70 years to accomplish his goal and thus determine his eternal rank for one hundred trillion years.

70 years to prepare for 100.000.000.000.000 years ! If then we use only 2 hours every day to prepare for one hundred trillion years and use 22 hours a day to do things that are of consequence only for the 70 years on earth, we would have shown ourselves to be most foolish. The wise person will

do all he can to invest more time working at what will matter beyond the seventy years.

The need to redeem time

if the time spent in this life will affect life in the other life very, very significantly, and if there are just 70 years in this life to prepare for one hundred trillion years, then every second in this life is of vital importance.

Taking the example above, 70 earthly years to prepare for 100.000.000.000.000 heavenly years.

1 earthly year to prepare for 1.428.571.000.000 heavenly years.

1 earthly day to prepare for 39.139.000.000 heavenly years.

1 earthly hour to prepare for 1.631.000.000 heavenly years.

Do you see what it means ? It means that if you waste one hour on earth, you have forfeited your opportunity to labour for blessings that will last not less than 1.631.000.000 eternity years! How true and how sad ! Do you realize it ?

Do you therefore see that each wasted minute amounts to a loss of at least 27.183.333 eternity years ?

My beloved brother, just face this fact: Every minute lost on earth amounts to the loss of an opportunity to contribute to that which will cover at the very least 27.183.333 eternity years.

If you allow someone to waste your one minute, you have allowed untold harm to be done to you. If you waste anyone's one minute, you have actually robbed him of 27.183.333 eternity years at the very least. Can you be so foolish to allow that to be done to you? Can you be so foolish to do that to yourself? Can you be so wicked to do that to another?

Since there is such a short time on earth to accomplish the call of God on our lives, it becomes absolutely necessary to redeem the time so as to better invest it. The Bible commands, *Look carefully then how you walk, not as unwise men but as wise making the most of the time, because the days are evil.* (Ephesians 5:15-16). The Psalmist prayed, *So teach us to number our days that we may get a heart of wisdom.* (Psalm 90:12).

The question might arise in your heart,"What can I do to make the most of the time ?" We suggest that you make the most of the time by adopting a war budget of time. We know that during times of war, war budgets are adopted in which things that are secondary are kept aside or given very little attention so that most of the finances are invested in the war. A war budget of time gives most of the time to accomplishing the goal of life. Soldiers have no time for some of the niceties of civilian life. We suggest the following budget of time to the one previously given:

1. Sleep(3 hours at night and one in the day)	4.0 hours
2. Personal hygiene	0.5 hour
3. Eating	1.0 hour
4. Relationships	1.5 hours
5. Unforeseen	0.5 hour

	7.5 hours

This is a gain of 6.5 hours which should all be invested into the one task of accomplishing your goal. This means that for a person who is working to earn his living and yet has the goal of his life to accomplish, there are 6.5 + 3.6 = 10.1 hours to invest in the task of accomplishing his life's goal.

Does it look unrealistic ? Certainly not. I know some people who are working on earning their living, who do a very good job at their "tent-making" but through rigorous discipline and sacrifice are investing an average of 12 hours into the Lord's call upon their lives daily.

Such people are bent on accomplishing their goal. They know how late the hour is

1. They work for eight hours a day from Monday to Friday afternoon.
2. They invest six hours every evening into their goal.
3. They sleep for 3 - 4 hours.
4. They invest 2 - 3 hours into their goal between 4 & 7 a:m every day.
5. They invest all Saturdays and Sundays into their goal.
6. They invest all public holidays into their goal.
7. They invest all their leave time into their goal.

Consequently, they invest an average of 12 hours every day into the Lord's service in the area of their goal every year.

You too can do the same.

You can discipline yourself.

You are not a failure.

Do not say that you are not able. You are able!

God will enable you to do it.

Pray saying, "Lord, enable me to live on a war budget of time and thereby discipline myself and invest an average of 12 hours a day into Your service from the near future on. I ask this in the name of the Lord Jesus. Amen."

6

Counting the cost.

The Lord Jesus asked that people count the cost before they embark on a project. We said that for your goal to be accomplished, you must put in your all. In the last chapter, we have shown the fact that you have to sacrifice your time. Before you continue, it will be good to face the cost.

Are you prepared to work about 18 hours a day ?

Are you prepared to invest your Saturdays and Sundays into your goal ?

Are you prepared to invest the hours between 4 a:m and 7 a:m into the accomplishment of your goal ?

Are you prepared to invest the time between 6 p:m and midnight into your goal ?

Are you prepared to divorce sleep and cut it to a minimum ?

Are you prepared to invest your Saturdays and Sundays into your goal ?

Are you prepared to invest all public holidays into your goal ?

Are you prepared to invest all your leave period into your goal?

Are you prepared to judge every person and every thing by its impact on your goal ?

Are you prepared to live and act like the communist who said, "There is one thing in which I am dead earnest and that is the Communist Cause. It is my life, my business, my religion, my hobby, my sweetheart, my wife, my mistress, my bread and my meat. I work at it in the day time and dream of it at night. Its hold on me grows, not lessens as time goes. Therefore, I cannot carry on a friendship, a love affair or even a conversation without relating it to this force which drives and guides my life. I evaluate people, books, ideas and actions according to how they affect the Communist Cause and by their attitude to it."

(From the book, "True Discipleship" by William Macdonald)

To live like him will cause you to be narrow,very narrow. Are you prepared for that? If you are not prepared for that, then you are not prepared to accomplish your goal.

You have to choose between your goal and sleep.

You have to choose between your goal and pleasure.

You have to choose between your goal and the company of men.

The cost of accomplishing one's goal as far as time is concerned is the investment of every

year

week

day

hour

minute and

second

of one's life into that activity or those activities that will enable the goal to be accomplished. For the use of every minute, the person who must succeed asks, "How can I invest this minute so that it enables me to accomplish my goal in the shortest possible time ?" When that question is asked, the cost has to be paid because a decision will have to be taken.

PRIORITIES

when the question is asked, things will fall into a number of classes that can be set forth as follows:

1. Those that will hinder the goal.
2. Those that will neither hinder the goal nor advance it.
3. Those that will advance the goal significantly.
4. Those that will advance the goal in a great way.
5. Those that will advance the goal in an indispensable way.
6. Those that will advance the goal in a most indispensable way.

To work hard in terms that we are using in this book is to invest all the time available in the things that are absolutely indispensable for the accomplishment of the project.

Are you prepared to give all your time to the prior issues of your goal, regardless of how you feel? Are you prepared to invest all your time into the doing of things that you may even find distasteful, provided they enable you to accomplish your goal?

UNLESS YOU ARE PREPARED TO COUNT THE COST IN THIS WAY, YOU SHOULD FORGET ABOUT YOUR GOAL. YOU WILL NEVER ACCOMPLISH IT . IF YOU DO NOT COUNT THE COST, YOU MAY START A PROJECT AND NEVER COMPLETE IT.

The Lord Jesus taught saying, "*For which of you desiring to build a tower, does not first sit down and count the cost, whether he has enough to complete it ? Otherwise, when he has laid a foundation and is not able to finish, those who see it begin to mock him saying, this man began to build, and was not able to finish.*" (Luke 14:28-30).

UNLESS YOU ARE PREPARED TO GET RID OF EVERYTHING THAT STANDS ON THE WAY OF YOUR GOAL, REGARDLESS OF HOW MUCH YOU LIKE IT, YOU WILL NOT BE ABLE TO ACCOMPLISH IT. COUNT THE COST !

7

The indispensable commitment.

You have decided, after counting the cost and weighing things all over, to accomplish the goal of your life. Your total being is willing. You are ready.

At this point, I recommend a three-fold commitment. First of all, I recommend you to commit yourself to yourself. It is better to write out your commitment. You can write it out as follows: "I,............, commit myself, spirit, soul and body to accomplish the goal of my life which is........... Evidence of the accomplishment of this goal will be the realization of the following projects:

1.

2.

3.

4.

I commit myself to accomplish that goal to the full satisfaction of the Lord God who has called me to it." Secondly, I recommend that you commit yourself to the Lord who called you and commissioned you. You can commit yourself to the Lord in the following words or in similar words: "My Lord and my God, I thank You for saving me and for calling me to serve You. I thank You for Your goal for my life which is............ I thank You for enabling me to break down that goal into the following projects, which when realized will be the realization of the project

1.

2.

3.

4.

Lord, I commit myself to put all that I am and all that I have into ensuring that the project is accomplished. Lord,I commit myself into putting all my time and all my energy, to ensure that the project is accomplished to Your perfect satisfaction. Lord, I am willing, help me. Lord, enable me to invest every ounce of my strength into the goal and never to look back. Lord, grant that I do it all for Your honour and glory and that I do not seek to draw attention to myself. In Jesus' name I ask. Amen."

The third thing is to commit yourself to some human being. There is in every human being a tendency to back out of things when things become very rough,

difficult,

boring.

At such moments, there is need for some stimulus from a brother or sister to keep us going. It is therefore important that you share your goal with someone. Tell him what you are going to accomplish and tell him to check on you. This will help. It is better if you give him a copy of your project and your commitment. It is better still if you publish what you intend to do in the assembly. Having published it, you are hooked before yourself, your God and the brethren. It will be difficult to withdraw.

I know moments when the road was very rough and the opposition fierce. The only reason why I kept going on with the goal that God has given me, was a "fear" of what to say to those to whom I had announced my goal. I confess that it would have been easier just to tell the Lord that I have failed. However, we know that in failure it is better to fall into the hands of the Lord than into the hands of man. So, because I could not get myself to fall into the hands of man, I was able to press on at the task until the difficult moment was over and the joy of serving my Lord again filled my being and made external stimuli unnecessary. I am that weak. You may be so much stronger that you do not need external stimuli. That is good. I recommend it to those who are as weak as myself. It will help them.

8

Transforming the goal into accomplishable projects.

If you are going to work hard in an intelligent way, you need to work out a number of projects which, when accomplished, will ensure that your goal is accomplished.

Take, for example, that God has asked you to evangelize a certain pagan tribe. You may possibly work out the following strategy:

Stage 01. Personal knowledge of the tribe.

Stage 02. Working out methods of communication.

Stage 03. Division of the tribe into five parts.

Stage 04. Evangelization of the first part.

Stage 05. Evangelization of the second part.

Stage 06. Evangelization of the third part.

Stage 07. Evangelization of the fourth part.

Stage 08. Evangelization of the fifth part.

Having worked out a plan, you can now invest your entire self into the project; but before you do that, you have to set down time limits. You should set out the date on which the project is to begin. Unless you set a date on which the project is to begin, you may never begin at all. There are three types of people on Planet Earth. One type, on seeing the goal, rush ahead and start it before they have worked out the plan. The second group never get started. They always find reasons to shift the issue into the future. They say, "We shall soon start." Since soon is very undefined, they never get anywhere or they start too late. In this way, they fail. The third class plans well, sets a date for starting and works hard to start on that day. We repeat that "they work hard to get started." Why do I say this? The reason is that the enemy will work hard to ensure that you rush ahead without planning or you remain one who plans indefinitely. He can attack you to ensure that you are always asking "How can I improve on the plan? Is there something that can be added? Is there something that can be subtracted?" There will always be things that can be added or subtracted and the ones that are immediately obvious upon seeking God about it should be. However, to spend one day after another planning is to make planning the goal and not a means to the goal.

If you are one who naturally hesitates, you should pray about it and seek to be set free by the Lord. There is a time to act ! When that time has come, to continue to "wait on the Lord" is to sin. It is to fail. It is using religious language to run away from working hard. It is laziness. So get started. You may find that that first step, the one to get started, is the most difficult. It is like a man getting out of the boat into the sea.

He loves the security of the boat. If he steps out, he will either swim (work hard) or drown.

I encourage you, hesitant brother, to get started.

You have planned and prepared enough.

Do not allow hesitation to ground your project.

Do not allow the fear of failure to destroy things for you.

Do not allow an analysis of past failures to deter you.

You are not alone!

God has asked you to work for Him.

He has asked you to work with Him.

He will work with you and if things become too rough, He will hold you and prevent you from drowning. Many people talk of Peter's lack of faith and his sinking. However, Peter had two experiences that the cowards in the boat never had. The first one is that he actually walked on the sea for some time. The others never walked on the sea, even one step. The second one is that he had the privilege of having the Lord rescue him from drowning. The others also missed that experience. It is better to try and fail than never to try at all. Better still is moving out with the Lord, and succeeding with him.

This inner unwillingness or hesitation is evidenced in many areas of life:

1. The unwillingness to take a decision.
2. The unwillingness to get out of bed when it is time to pray.
3. The unwillingness to stop talking and start praying.

4. The unwillingness to stop reading the Bible and start praying.
5. The unwillingness to start talking to that person about salvation.
6. The unwillingness to face the person and say *"You have sinned"*.
7. The unwillingness to actually carry the dirt away.
8. The unwillingness to stop playing and start the lesson.
9. The unwillingness to open the mouth and start confessing your sin.

These are the characteristics of the lazy. The Bible admonishes them, *Go to the ant, O sluggard; consider her ways and be wise. Without having any chief, officer or ruler, she prepares her food in summer, and gathers her sustenance in harvest. How long will you lie there, O sluggard? When will you arise from your sleep ? A little sleep, a little slumber a little folding of the hands to rest, and poverty will come upon you like a vagabond and want like an armed man.* (Proverbs 6:6-11).

For every project or action, there is a critical point beyond which correct action becomes either very difficult or impossible ! There is that additional five minutes of sleep which when desired, may result in two or three hours of more sleep and two or three hours lost for prayer ! There is an indecision that could affect your destiny or that of another eternally. Be sure to act and to act on time. Do they not say, "Hit the iron while it is still hot"?

Let me be personal with you: What have you always postponed ?

Is it some sin to depart from ?

Is it some righteousness to commit ?

Is it some restitution to carry out ?

Is it some bad habit to abandon ?

Is it some relationship to start ?

Is it some letter to write ?

Is it a letter that has been written and needs to be put into an envelope ?

Is it an address that needs to be written on the envelope ?

Is it an offer of love that you need to make?

Is it an act of forgiveness that you need to carry out ?

Listen, you have waited enough. Go right now. Stop reading the next sentence and either do what you ought to have done or begin to do it.

Setting time limits

when you have worked out your plan, you need to set time limits. There should be a date set before which each stage must be completed. To do this, the date of starting and terminating the project needs to be set. God does not call someone to evangelize a certain tribe eternally. The tribe must be evangelized before a certain date. There is perhaps no greater incentive to hard work than time limits. When a person gives himself a time limit before God, he has put himself under pressure. For example, he may say, "Lord, I discern that You want me to start the evangelization of this town on 1st March

1989 and be through by December 31st 1992." Having made that commitment, the person should consider it as a vow unto the Lord. There is no way he can get out of it. There is now a transaction between him and the Lord. He believes the Lord and the Lord believes him. On or before December 31st 1992, that village should be presented to the Lord, fully evangelized in the way that satisfies the heart. That is hard work.

So there will be a date for starting and a date for the completion of each stage. Dealing thus with God, the fear of God, the fear of failing Him, the fear of losing the reward, the fear of having one's reward taken by another, will all combine into a force that will cause the person to :

- labour,
- press on,
- toil,
- sweat,
- buffet his body,
- endure pain,
- sacrifice sleep,
- sacrifice pleasure,
- sacrifice everything else,
- take no rest,
- give God no rest,
- accept all God-sent help,
- keep the eye only at the goal,
- keep oneself only at the job, until all is finished and presented to the Lord of glory.

The Lord actually calls people to take no rest and give Him no rest. He says, *Upon your walls, O Jerusalem, I have set watchmen; all the day and all the night they shall never be silent. You who put the Lord in remembrance, take no rest and give him no rest until he establishes Jerusalem and makes it a praise in the earth.* (Isaiah 62:6-7).

It could be that something that you expected would take three months is actually delayed and it takes four months. You may also find that another thing that was planned for three months actually takes two months. These things do happen. The result of this is that the dates for the termination of various phases of the project need not be final but only directional. The unnegotiable factor is when the finished project will be handed over to the One who asked it to be done !

Glory be to His holy name! Amen.

Someone has said "The only way to eat an elephant is to take a mouthful at a time and soon it will all be gone."

Another said, "In a journey of one thousand kilometres, the most difficult step is the first."

On the job working hard.

1

Keeping the goal in view always.

A fanatic is a person who, having lost sight of his goal, redoubles his effort to get there. The fanatic runs around frantically getting nowhere. He is a basketball player without a basket, a tennis player without a net, a golfer without a green.

(R.C Sproul in "Pleasing God." Tyndale House Publishers, Inc. Wheaton, Illinois, 1988).

It is possible to start with a clear goal and lose the goal somewhere along the line. This too easily happens since the fiercest attacks of Satan are directed against the goal; the vision. He knows too well that the goal can be lost, and yet a person keeps working hard, going nowhere. Such a person will rejoice and pride himself in the fact that he is working hard, but he will not ask where the hard work is taking him to.

There are house wives who labour so hard to please their husbands. They work at doing the things that they did ten years ago, but do not seem to come any nearer pleasing the men. They fail to realize that the men have grown and the things that pleased them ten years ago no longer satisfy. In a sense, these wives are like fanatics. They will end up being frustrated.

Another illustration is that of a man who sets out to write a book about the return of the Lord. He is so caught up with writing the book that he allows his relationship with the Lord to deteriorate so much that at the return of the Lord he is so busy writing his book that he hardly hears the trumpet sound.

There are some things that must be done to ensure that purposeless energy is not exerted. Some things must be done to ensure that the hard work remains directed towards the initial goal. These include:

1. The goal should be kept at a place where it is easily accessible. It should be written in a Bible or any such place.
2. The goal should be read at least once a week. It should preferably be read every day.
3. All the projects being carried out in order to enable the goal to be accomplished should constantly be reviewed so as to ensure that they do not become the goal but a means to the goal.
4. Any project that is found no longer necessary for the accomplishment of the goal should be abandoned at once.
5. Nothing should be done because it was done in the past.
6. Nothing should be considered useful because it was considered useful in the past.
7. The activities that are priority need to be evaluated from time to time.
8. Much prayer needs to be invested in order to ensure that the vision is protected from the attacks of Satan.

9. The devil needs to be attacked before he attacks the vision.
10. The peace of God in the inner man needs to be checked from time to time. Those who have lost the vision can become so given to hard work, going nowhere, that they become restless and frantic.
11. Much prayer should be invested to ensure that the project remains in the centre of God's will. The great problem is that many hard-working people have no spiritual sensitivity. They are so lost in working hard that although they received the initial information from the Lord correctly, they have since no longer heard from Him. They are like a pilot who correctly received take-off instructions, knew his destination, but after take-off, lost contact with the control tower. He will most probably crash.

In order to avoid all this, WORK HARD AT THE PROJECT AND WORK HARD AT KEEPING THE GOAL IN VIEW.

2

The importance of records.

Those who work hard and those who plan to work hard keep accurate records of where they are investing their energies. They do not just go on hoping that all would be alright.

A serious turn in my prayer life came when I decided to keep a record of how much time I was spending in prayer. Before that time I used to pray and truly believed that I was a man of prayer. I decided to record the exact time during which I prayed each time, recording the exact time at which I started praying and at which I stopped praying. I did this for a week which was normal and was shocked when I made the totals for each day and for the entire week. I had prayed for one-third of the amount of time I thought I was praying. I was shocked. What had happened ?

SELF DECEPTION

I thought I was praying much whereas I was not. My thoughts or imaginations were very far removed from reality. I was self-deceived. These facts forced me to repent, carry out restitution and begin to make progress in prayer. I then decided that I would keep a record of how I was using my time each day. My record shows what the time was used for from the moment I woke up to the moment I went to bed each night. A glance at the way I am spending my time easily shows what the goal or the priorities of my life are. I can no longer be deceived about whether or not I am putting time into my goal. Figures are revealing.

Do not be self-deceived

You too may be as self-deceived as I was. The only way out is to keep an honest record of how your time is being used. It will shock you but it will enable you to face facts, repent and change. It will require discipline, but discipline is an integral part of hard work.

Because you will be recording exactly how you are spending your time and not how you think you are spending it, you will not put your time into things that you will not be proud of. You will, for example, love to see on record that you spent many hours in prayer, few hours in sleeping, eating and the like. Because that is what you would want recorded, you will labour to bring it to pass so that your record may be true. In this way you have another incentive to work hard.

Accountability

God ordained accountability. The Bible says, *For we must all appear at the judgment seat of Christ, so that each one may receive good or evil according to what he has done in the body*. (II Corinthians 5:10). The Lord told the parable of the talents in which the master on return, settled accounts with them. (Matthew 25:14-

30). We shall ultimately give account to the Lord of the way in which we spent each

……...	minute

ounce of energy

franc

opportunity

that He gave us from birth until we meet Him. This serves as a stimulus to hard work now. However, no one needs to wait until then to learn and to practise the art of being accountable. It may be too late then. The wise person learns and practises accountability now in order not to be deceived. He also practises accountability so that he may be forced to press on and be his best.

So, the wise person puts himself under someone to whom he is accountable. All who reject this will not make all the progress that they could make. Those who are already doing very well without being accountable to someone on earth, could certainly do better if they placed themselves under someone to whom they were accountable. Those who are doing averagely or poorly could each do better if they were accountable to someone.

Why is that so? I believe that God has put into each human being a desire to want to be approved. He Himself will judge us to approve or to disapprove us. Because of this desire to be approved that God has put into us, when a person is accountable to someone, he will seek to be approved by the person to whom he is accountable. He will not want to be disapproved of. He will consequently do all he can to be approved. As far as hard work is concerned, the one seeking to be approved will :

work hard,

work harder,

work harder and harder,

and work hardest, in order to continue to be approved.

The other side of the matter is that the one to whom we are accountable will encourage us when we need encouragement and help us to see things clearly if things have become blurred because we have lost the vision.

CHOICE OF A PERSON TO WHOM TO BE ACCOUNTABLE

in order that the art of accountability may make sense and help you to work hard, the person to whom you decide to be accountable should normally have all or most of the following qualifications:

1. He should know the Lord Jesus as his Lord and Saviour.
2. He should be radically committed to the Lord Jesus.
3. He should be a person who has a long-standing history of working hard.
4. He should be thoroughly honest and thus, able to call a spade a spade.
5. He should love you deeply.
6. He should not fear you, that is; he should be able to tell you the truth readily.

7. He should hold you in high esteem.
8. He should believe that you are where God wants you to be.
9. He should have the authority to rebuke you.
10. He should have the capacity to see hidden flaws.
11. He should have the ability to inspire you and congratulate you.
12. He should have the power to lift you up when you are discouraged and help you to move on.
13. He should be available for personal contact, preferably once a month.
14. He should be a person you do not want to fail or let down or hurt.

It could be that you do not find someone with many of these characteristics. You can still be accountable. You should then choose someone who is where you are and you should decide to be mutually accountable to each other. That failing, do not give up. Choose someone who is below you and regularly show him what you set out to do and what you have actually done.

What must you do with the person to whom you are accountable? We make the following suggestions:

1. You should know that it is for your good that he decides to have you accountable to him.
2. You should treat him with high respect and encourage him from time to time by some token of gratitude or the other.
3. You should discuss what you are investing yourself into with him.

4. You should let him have a copy of your goals and the time limits for accomplishing each one of them.
5. You should be totally honest with him so that he knows the facts and not imaginations.
6. You should be prepared to receive a rebuke if that is what you deserve.
7. You should seek him and not wait for him to look for you. Remember, it is the patient who seeks the physician.
8. You should prepare things and be orderly when you go to see him.
9. You should not waste his time.
10. You should not bring in things that are outside the evaluation of your progress.
11. You should show him the details of how you have used each day that month.
12. You should spell out how much time was invested into your goal.
13. You should spell out how much work was done.
14. You should spell out how much time was wasted.
15. You should tell him your evaluation of the way you worked: if it was very hard,

    hard,

    not hard enough,

    lazy.

16. You should tell him if you think you are able on your own to improve on your performance without any help from him.

17. You should spell out to what extent you think you can improve on your performance.
18. You should tell him where you think your problem lies.
19. You should be quiet and let him think through.
20. You should listen as he speaks.
21. You should ask questions.
22. You should agree together on the goal to be accomplished before the next appointment.
23. You should repent to God and to him for any faults or failures that resulted from laziness.
24. You should thank him for correcting you.
25. You should pray together before you leave.
26. You should go away determined to do better by working harder,regardless of whether you were praised or rebuked.
27. Praise the Lord!

3

The power of pressure: being stirred up.

The story is told of a man who was badly wounded in a primitive inter-tribal war. He was so badly wounded that he could not walk, not to say anything about running. He was so badly wounded that his companions carried him on a stretcher and were retreating with him. Soon they heard gunshots at short range from the pursuing enemy. They then said to the wounded man, "Since you are wounded and may soon die, it is not good that the enemy should come and kill all of us. We will leave you here and run for our lives." They were surprised when the man said, "Put me down and let me see what I can do." They put him down and to their amazement, he did not only walk but ran almost as fast as those who were not wounded.

God has given each one power that can be released in an emergency. It is quite certain that if a poor runner were being chased by a lion, he might run at a speed that would break many world records. Do you not believe? I believe it. Every person does his best under pressure. Under pressure, people have worked tirelessly for days. Under pressure, people have gone without sleep for days. Under pressure, the impossible has been made possible.

If the one to whom you are accountable helps to put you under pressure, he would have served a useful purpose. There is no question about the fact that if you hold him in high honour, you will work hard throughout the month. You will certainly work harder the third week and hardest the fourth week if you lost the first week or if your goal was so high that it could not be accomplished by normal work.

It would have been alright to have only the Lord Jesus as the One to whom we are accountable in time. The problem is that none of us or very few of us ever attain that degree of spirituality. We therefore need each other. The Bible says, *And let us consider how to stir up one another to love and good works.* (Hebrews 10:24).

You need another person to stir you up to good works. You need someone to stir you to work

hard work

harder work

hardest work.

Look for him and let him help you! Begin today.

The wicked stir people up beyond measure. They stir others up to do the things they want. They excite beyond measure in such a way that action is inevitable. The Bible says, *But the Jews incited the devout women of high standing and the leading men of the city, and stirred up opposition against Paul and Barnabas, and drove them out of their district.* (Acts 13:50). The Bible again says,

But the unbelieving Jews stirred up the Gentiles and poisoned up their minds against the brethren. (Acts 14:2).

What these unbelievers did to stir people up against the Gospel shows clearly that man has something in him that can be stirred up into action. Look for someone who can stir you up to action for the accomplishment of your God-given goal.

Talk with people who are giving all of themselves to the accomplishment of God's call on their lives. What you hear will stir you up. As you are stirred up, you will be under pressure and you will act, working hard.

PRAY THAT THE LORD SHOULD STIR YOU UP

the Lord can stir people up to action. The Bible says, "In the first year of Cyrus King of Persia, that the word of the Lord by the mouth of Jeremiah might be accomplished, the Lord stirred up the spirit of Cyrus King of Persia so that he made a proclamation throughout all his kingdom and also put it into writing: *Thus says Cyrus King of Persia: The Lord, the God of heaven, has given me all the kingdoms of the earth, and he has charged me to build him a house at Jerusalem, which is in Judah.* (Ezra 1:1).

The Lord stirred up the heart of this pagan king, causing him to do that which he could normally not do. He can do the same for you. Have you cried to Him in prayer saying, "Lord, stir my heart up that I might be able to do all Your will with all of my heart, with all of my soul, and with all of my might"? If you have never prayed like that , why not pray like that now for the first time? Why not continue to pray like that every day? Why not continue to pray like that until the Lord has stirred you so mightily that you will not help working with all your might ? Why don't you continue praying like that until all of your being is set on fire to please the Lord so much that nothing can stand in the way of your putting every thing you are and all your energy into doing God's will? The Lord has promised to answer the prayers of His children. He says, *If you ask anything in my name, I will do it.* (John 14:14). Please, ask and it will be done unto you.

The Bible says, *And the Lord stirred up the spirit of Zerubbabel the son of Shealtiel, governor of Judah, and the spirit of Joshua the son of Jehozadak, the high priest and the spirit of all the remnant of the people, and they came and worked on the house of the Lord of hosts, their God.* (Haggai 1:14).

These people worked on the house of the Lord because the Lord stirred their hearts up. He will do the same to you if you believe, ask and continue asking.

It is then obvious that you can be stirred up by the Lord to do His will or stirred up by the enemy to do the enemy's will.

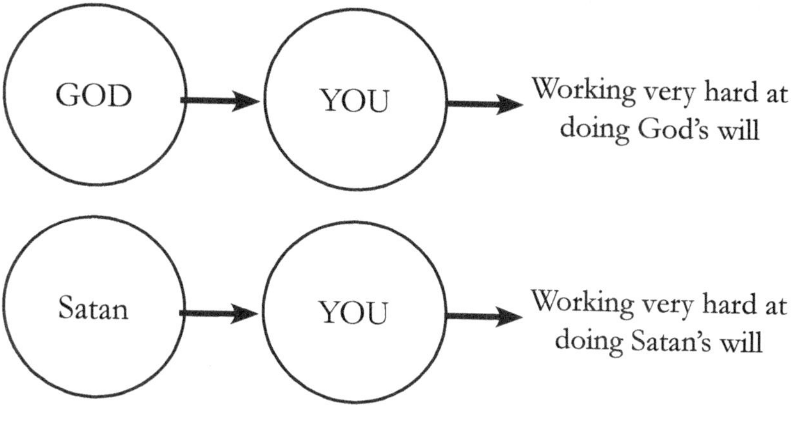

Early in Paul's life, he was stirred up by Satan to oppose the Lord Jesus and His Church. Later on, he was stirred up by the Holy Spirit to labour totally for the Lord Jesus. Being stirred up by the Holy Spirit, the Bible says, *Now while Paul was waiting for them at Athens, his spirit was provoked within him as he saw that the city was full of idols. So he argued in the synagogue with the Jews and devout persons, and in the market place every day with those who chanced to be there.* (Acts 17:16). Paul was provoked, stirred up in the spirit by the Lord. The Lord used the instrumentality of what he saw to stir his spirit up, and as his spirit was being stirred up, he acted on a daily basis. The stirring was not a passing emotion. It was permanent. It continued with continued action.

The Lord will stir up those who are already stirring themselves up to work for Him. He will stir them up so that they can work harder and harder for His glory.

On the other hand, the devil will stir those who are idle. He will stir them to become aflame with passion to serve him and to do his will. It is important that you stir yourself up to do God's will so that the Lord will further stir you up to do His will.

4

The power of pressure: stirring yourself up

We have shown that the Lord does stir people up. We have similarly shown that Satan can stir people up. We have shown that the Lord stirs those who stir themselves.

People can stir themselves up to action. The prophet Isaiah complained, *There is none that calls upon thy name, that bestirs himself to take hold on thee.* (Isaiah 64:7). Timothy was encouraged by Paul to rekindle (stir up) the gift of God that was in him. (II Timothy 1:6). Even the Lord of heaven was exhorted: *Stir up thy might, and come to save us*! (Psalms 80:20). The Bible says, *And Moses called Bezalel and Oholiab and every able man in whose heart the Lord had put ability, every one whose heart stirred him up to come to do the work.* (Exodus 36:2).

The question then might arise, "How can I stir myself up?" There are a number of things that you should do in order to stir yourself up.

1. Walk very close to the Lord. If you walk close to the Lord, your spirit will be stirred up within you as a result of your close walk with Him. If you commit sin, your spirit will become dampened and it will not be able to

rise up to any real action for the Lord. Rather, the enemy might take over and stir you up to serve him. There is no substitute to holiness in working hard for the Lord. If you were working hard for the devil, holiness would be unnecessary, but because you are God's child and working for Him, He commands you to be holy even as He is holy.

2. Read the Word. The things you read will affect you. Read the Word of God. That is the second way to stir yourself up. As you read and meditate, you will become saturated with the Word and that will lead to action. Also read books that talk about bold action for the Lord. Read the biographies of people who worked hard for the Lord. You can first of all read the biographies of men of the Bible as you read the Bible and see how they worked hard at doing great things for God. Abraham, David, Joshua, Caleb, Moses, Paul etc. Then you should read the biographies of people who did great things for God: Martin Luther, John Wesley, Charles Wesley, Jonathan Edward, Watchman Nee, John Sung, Hudson Taylor, C.T. Studd, just to name a few. As you read with an open heart and with prayer that the Lord should enable you to stir yourself up to work very hard for Him, He will do it

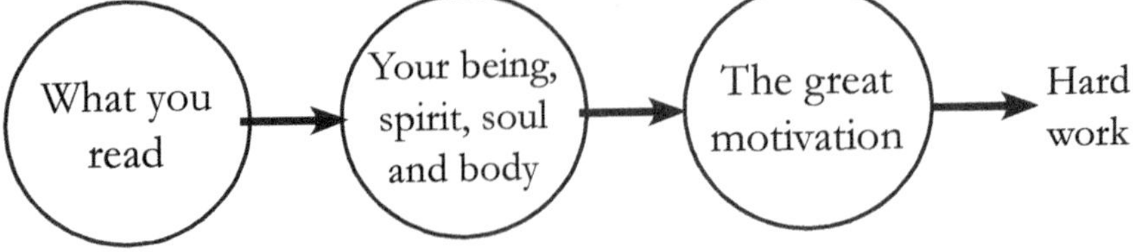

3. Get close to hard-working people. Live with them and see them at work. What you see will affect your actions. What you gaze at will have an impact on you. Cultivate

the friendship of a hard-working person. Get very close to him. See how he goes about things. Find out his secret and imitate him.

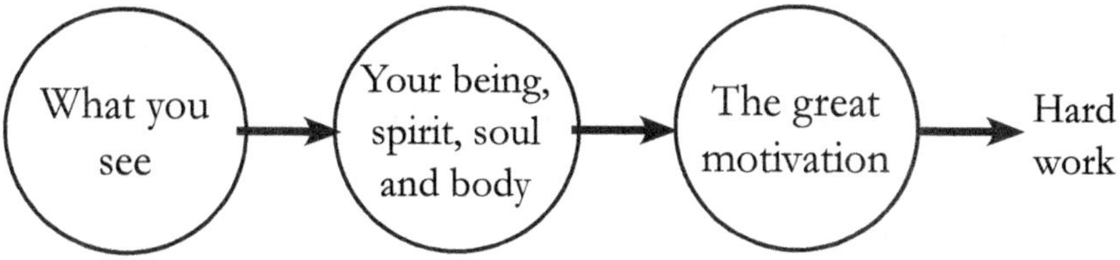

4. Practise what you already know about hard work. Do not be a person who is only a hearer of the Word. Be a doer also. Do not be one who is always learning but never coming to the knowledge of the truth. Unless you begin to use the knowledge that you have already acquired, you are likely to block yourself from further knowledge.
5. Write out your goal and put it in many places. Put it near your bed. Put it behind the door in your bedroom. Put a copy in your sitting room. Put a copy in your office. Put a copy in your Bible. Put a copy near your dining table. Put a copy in your car. Put copies in all other places which will help you to confront it many times a day.
6. Write statements like the following and put them around.
7. I must accomplish my goal.
8. I must work hard.
9. Jesus worked hard. I must imitate Him and therefore work hard.
10. The Lord will reward hard work.
11. The Lord promotes hard-working people.
12. I must work hard in order not to bury my talent(s).
13. The minute before me is precious. I must not waste it. I must invest it into my God-given goal.

14. The minute before me is perishable. I must redeem it by working hard.
15. I refuse to work very hard. I will work extremely hard.
16. Hard work is one of the ways into God's heart.
17. People respect hard-working people.
18. I must, by hard work, set a good example before my children.
19. I will meet the minutes before me again on Judgment Day. I must use them with all my might so that when I see them on that day, I shall rejoice in and with my Lord.
20. God is taking a film of my life moment by moment. I must work hard throughout so that as He sees the film of my life, He will rejoice in the victory of Christ.
21. The people whose lives are examples for me all worked hard. I will be like them.
22. The Lord is stirring me up to work hard. I respond.
23. The Lord is inviting me to hard work. I will obey.
24. There is work to do now. I will not leave it for the next minute.
25. There is joy in working hard.
26. John Wesley worked hard and lived to be eighty-eight years, full of strength in his old age.
27. Caleb worked hard and did great exploits in old age.
28. The apostle Paul worked harder than the other apostles and consequently wrote almost half of the books of the New Testament.
29. I will work hard because my Lord is seeing me even if no one else is seeing me.

30. I must work hard so as to contribute to the salvation of the lost. I refuse to be guilty of the blood of anyone through laziness.
31. I am being prepared here for rulership with Christ in His Kingdom. I will work very hard as practice.
32. I will work hard now and always so that praise may go up to my heavenly Father.
33. I will work extremely hard so as to frustrate the devil's purposes.
34. Put these things into practice. Begin now.

5

The pathway to permanent greatness.

One danger that a person faces in the course of working hard for the Lord and pressing on to accomplish the call of God in his life, is that he could easily turn his eyes off the Lord as he concentrates on the work. The result of this will be that he will remove the Lord (sometimes unconsciously) from the centre of the work and deify himself. This is tragic beyond telling; for he will begin to labour, not for the glory of the Lord, but for his own glory. He will receive the glory for the work and his speech will increasingly abound with "I, I, my, me, me" etc.

There are some things to bear in mind so as to avoid this tragedy from occurring. There are some things to do so as to prevent it.

The first thing to bear in mind is that God is the Author of the work. You cannot bring anything into existence. The apostle Paul said, *Last of all, as to one untimely born, he appeared to me. For I am the least of the apostles, unfit to be called an apostle because I persecuted the Church of God. But by the grace of God, I am what I am, and his grace toward me was not in vain. On the contrary, I worked harder than any of them, though it was not I, but the grace of God which is in me.* (I Corinthians 15:8-10).

Let us look at the phrases that the apostle Paul used in these three verses:

1. Last of all.
2. As to one untimely born He appeared to me.
3. I am the least of the apostles.
4. Unfit to be called an apostle.
5. I persecuted the Church of God.
6. By the grace of God, I am what I am.
7. His grace toward me was not in vain.
8. I worked harder than any of them though it was not I.
9. But the grace of God which is in me.

There is no question that Paul put the Lord Jesus and His grace at the centre. He showed his own failure and gave credit for his hard work, not to himself, but to Another--the Lord Jesus and His grace.

Decide that you will never give credit for the product of the work you have done to yourself. If you see any tendency towards this, fight it vehemently through repentance and heart-cry to God. Plead with God daily that He should deliver you and your work for Him from your worst enemy--yourself, that is, the self in you that wants to show off.

Decide that you will not woo, expect and receive the praise from men for the work you have done for the Lord. Refuse to be praised. Constantly do these things:

1. Show your own failures that have hindered the work from reaching higher heights than have been attained or from going faster than it has gone.
2. Tell people plainly that God did it and that you were a mere instrument in His hands and that if He had chosen to use another, the work would possibly have been better and moved faster.
3. Move away from those who want to praise you. If you cannot move away, rebuke them sharply so that the story will soon go around that any one who praises you will have a bad time.
4. Exalt others who worked with you whom people do not know about.
5. Run away to a lonely place and pray.

The second thing to bear in mind is that even though you have worked hard, things have succeeded because of the grace of God. There are people who have worked harder than you and failed to produce the same results. Had God not stepped in, it could have been said of you, *Now therefore, thus says the Lord of hosts: Consider how you have fared. You have sown much and harvested little; you eat, but you never have enough, you drink, but you never have your fill; you clothe yourselves, but no one is warm; and he who earns wages earns them to put them in a bag with holes.* (Haggai 1:5-6). *You have looked for much, and, lo, it came to little; and when you brought it home, I blew it away.* (Haggai 1:9). *Therefore the heavens above you have withheld the dew, and the earth has withheld its produce. And I called for a drought upon the land and the hills, upon the grain, the new wine and the oil, upon what the ground brings forth, upon men and cattle and upon all their labours.* (Haggai 1:10-11) However, the Lord stepped in and blessed you and your efforts and He should be given the credit and the glory for it. I dare say that He should be given all the credit for it. God was at work in you both to will and to do His good pleasure. (Philippians 2:13). Without Him you would have been nothing and you would have done nothing. You do not have anything which you did not receive from Him.

We are not saying that you did not work. We are only saying that you worked because He was at work in you both to will and to do His good pleasure. We are insisting that the glory, all the glory, should go to Him without whom you are nothing. We are only saying that all you are and did fits well with the apostle's proclamation, *So it depends not upon man's will or exertion but upon God's mercy.* (Romans 9:16).

You will receive your reward when He comes. You are even now being rewarded by being granted the privilege to be used. Rejoice in the fact that you have been used. Rejoice and give the glory to Him. Some day, you will wear a crown and reign with Him. For now, let Him have all the honour. As you honour Him, giving Him all the honour and glory for your accomplishments, He will in turn exalt you and give you more opportunities to serve Him.

The third thing to bear in mind is that, if you allow pride to come into your heart, it will be to your undoing. The Scriptures say, *Those who walk in pride, He is able to abase.* (Daniel 4:37). He brings down the proud of heart and exalts the humble. I pray that your attitude be like that of Daniel who told King Nebuchadnezzar, *But as for me, not because of any wisdom that I have more than all the living, has this mystery been revealed to me, but in order that the interpretation may be made known to the King, and that you may know the thoughts of your mind.* (Daniel 2:20).

You are a co-worker with God. The apostle Paul said, *Working together with him, then, we entreat you not to accept the grace of God in vain.* (II Corinthians 6:1). He again said, *For we are God's fellow workers.* (I Corinthians 3:9). As a co-worker then, it is obvious that God is the Senior Partner.

The work is His.

The plan of it is His.

He called you to it.

He gave you all the enabling.

He enabled you to work hard.

He enabled you to press on to the end.

He deserves all the praise.

Keep giving Him all the praise; keep allowing Him to have the first place and you will soon find that as you exalt Him, He carries you with Him into great heights of honour and eternal glory, heights that you could never attain on your own.

That is the pathway to permanent greatness.

Glory be to Him!

6

Faint but pursuing.

There are moments in the accomplishment of any task that the hard-working person gets to the end or almost the last bit of his energy, both physical and emotional. It is as if he should just drop everything and rest. He has worked very hard and considerable progress has been made. By every standard of assessment, he has been faithful and he has put himself truly into it. He is also aware that to stop the work then and have some rest may ruin the entire project or a part of it. What then is he to do?

I believe that there is only one answer. He must keep pressing on. If you are in that situation, you may be faint but you must keep pursuing the course you have followed in the past. You must just press on.

Remember what you have already put into the project. Can you afford to lose it? I am not saying that you are not tired. I am only asking if you have counted the cost of stopping and having a break at the moment. You have the choice before you. Choose to press on even though you are tired.

You can press on even though you are tired. There are extra energy reserves hidden inside you that will be released when you decide that the project must be finished without further postponing of it. Listen to what the Bible says : *Have you not known ? Have you not heard ? The Lord is the everlasting God, the Creator of the ends of the earth. He does not faint or grow weary, His understanding is unsearchable. He gives power to the faint, and to him who has no might he increases strength. Even youths shall faint and be weary, and young men shall fall exhausted ; but they who wait for the Lord shall renew their strength, they shall mount up with wings like eagles, they shall run and not be weary, they shall walk and not faint.* (Isaiah 40:28-31).

These verses are addressed to you, weary faint worker. The Lord for whom and with whom you are working does not grow faint or weary. He started working with you. You are faint but He is not. You are weary but He is strong. You no longer understand, but His own understanding is full and fresh. You can count on Him. Say to Him, "Lord, I am faint, but you are not; I am weary but you are not. I will not count on my faintness or weariness. I will count on your strength and your freshness now. Lord, make Your strength and your freshness available for me now."

As you turn to him that way, believe Him. He has heard you and He is answering you right now. You should continue working, pressing on. Your situation is surely one which even youths (people who have not yet invested their strength into work) may not be able to cope with. They might soon grow faint and weary. However, as you look to the Lord, continue to work, you will find that your strength is being renewed by a flow that comes from the Lord. The strength of the One who does not grow weary is being made available to you through His Spirit Who dwells in you. You will find that you have become so strong that you are able to fly into spiritual heights like an eagle in the project. You will be able to run in the accomplishment of the project and not be weary and also walk and not faint. You will find that God's strength has become so perfect for you in weakness that you are able to press on with the work. The apostle Paul confessed, *When I am weak, then I am strong.* (II Corinthians 12:10). He was saying, "When I am weak, the Lord makes me strong." He will do that for you.

There is also one thing to further bear in mind. If you say that you have come to the end of your strength and nothing can be done for you, things are likely to be as you have created with your words. The Lord warned the children of Israel, *If you say in your heart, These nations are greater than I; how can I dispose them ? You shall not be afraid of them but you shall remember what the Lord your God did to Pharaoh and to all Egypt.* (Deuteronomy 7:17-18).

So when you are faint, weak and weary, do not shout, "I am weary; I am faint, and I am weary and done for." Rather, you should confess aloud, " The Lord will satisfy my weary soul and replenish my languishing being. He will do it and is doing it even now. (Jeremiah 31:25).

Confess, *The Lord is the strength of his people.* (Psalm 28:8).

God is our refuge and strength. (Psalm 46:1).

The Lord is my refuge and my song. (Psalm 118:14).

The Lord is my strength and my song. (Exodus 15:2).

The Lord is my strength and my song. (Isaiah 12:2).

Keep confessing the Lord as your strength and you will never be the same.

You will remember that the Lord Jesus was tired and weary and needed food, which the disciples went to buy. He waited at Jacob's well. As the woman of Samaria came, He did not continue in weariness. Rather, He turned to His Father and received strength from above, and with it ministered. When the disciples brought food, He was no longer waiting for it. He had been fed from above and left them wondering, "Has any one brought Him food ?"

Indeed, someone had brought Him food--the heavenly Father. That someone is available; He is your co-worker. He will bring you food. Turn to Him and be refreshed. Turn even now. He is waiting to minister to you. Turn now and receive ministry and then go on.

Some practical tips

there are some tips that a tired or sleepy person could apply to himself so as to continue working. If he is sleepy, he should walk around the house or go outside and walk around and even run. He will return strong and freed from sleep.If he continues to be sleepy, he should fill a large basin with cold water and put it under his desk, put his feet inside and sleep will fly away, and thus leave him to read, write, study or do any other work which can be done while the body is in that position. My beloved father used this technique very often and I have, myself, used it when other methods to keep awake while pressing on failed.

For the tired person who is not sleepy, eating a fruit or drinking a glass of juice or milk will strengthen the body, renew the strength and make continued work possible. Amen.

7

A finished task.

There are many people who started on the Christian Way and soon gave up! There are many who went to school but did not finish the course. There are many who started a relationship and left it unconsummated. There are many who started to build a house and stopped :

- at the foundation
- at the walls
- at the roof
- etc.

There are many who started to write a book but stopped short of finishing it! One can go on and on with examples of people who started good projects but did not finish them. Every person who has decided to work as a co-worker with God must decide that he will complete the projects that he starts. I know of a man who has four houses but none is completed. He can neither live in any of them nor give one out for rents. He hasn't got any money left to continue building either.

God is not like that. The Bible says, *And God saw everything that he had made and behold it was very good. And there was evening and there was morning, a sixth day. Thus the heavens and the earth were finished, and all the host of them. And on the seventh day, God finished his work which he had done and he rested on the seventh day from all his work which he had done.* (Genesis 1:31-2:2). So, we see that God finished His work.

The Lord Jesus finished His work. From the cross, He proclaimed, "*It is finished.*" After that, He gave His Spirit to His Father. All through His life, He was burdened to finish His work that the Father had given Him to do. He put all of Himself into it and told the Father towards the end, *I glorified thee on earth, having accomplished the work which thou gavest me to do.* (John 17:4).

The apostle Paul was given work to do by the Lord Jesus. He gave himself to it and said, *I do not account my life of any value nor as precious to myself, if only I may accomplish my course and the ministry which I received from the Lord Jesus, to testify to the Gospel of the grace of God.* (Acts 20:24).

You too must labour at finishing the task that He has given you. The Lord Jesus glorified the Father by accomplishing the work that the Father gave Him to do. That is the way you too can glorify the Father. Does it not mean that uncompleted tasks do not glorify Him ? Does it not mean that uncompleted tasks bring shame to Him? Can you afford to bring shame to His name through uncompleted tasks?

In order to finish the work and accomplish your goal, do the following:

1. Decide that you must finish the work before you.
2. Remind yourself that there is no reward for uncompleted tasks.

3. Remind yourself that a task that is 90% completed is incomplete and therefore not fit for a reward.
4. Decide that you will labour to keep to the date for finishing the task.
5. Decide that you will not start another project until the present one is truly finished.
6. Decide that finishing does not mean the completion of the general structure, but the fitting in of all the fine details, as God is also concerned about details.
7. Decide that you will not allow anyone to persuade you to stop short of completing the work.
8. Decide that you will be patient with the fine details. These take a lot of time and may not be as interesting as the gross structure. To patiently press on with one detail after another until all has been done is a mark of maturity in working hard. While brute force in working hard can get the gross structure done, refined hard work will get the fine details to be fitted in. The successful person will be involved with both.
9. When you think that you have finished, look at it carefully. Is it really finished ? Are there no loopholes ? Can it be presented to God as it is ? You may, in the course of inspecting the thing and asking these questions, find that there are some details that need to be fitted in. Work at them. When you are satisfied, thank the Lord and,
10. Ask the person to whom you are accountable to come and evaluate it. He will come and evaluate it. If he shows you things that need to be done, do them. If he says that it is completed, then you can present the project to God.

11. Do not leave it uncompleted because there are obstacles that cannot easily be surmounted. Labour at surmounting them. Do not leave it uncompleted because it can be used as it is. It can indeed be used by you or by others, but the Lord will not use that which can be completed but which is not completed. Do not leave it uncompleted because it has cost you so much time and so much energy and you have done better than others. Even if you have done better than others, do better still by completing it. Remember that others may not complete theirs but you must complete yours. That is the way to God's heart.
12. Praise the Lord for having been faithful. Amen.

Examples of believers who worked hard.

1

The apostle paul and hard work.

The apostle Paul worked hard. We shall quote just a few passages from his writing to illustrate this. At the beginning of his union with Christ, Ananias told him, "*The God of our fathers appointed you to know his will, to see the Just One and to hear a voice from his mouth; for you will be a witness for him to all men of what you have seen and heard.*" (Acts 22:14-15). To him personally, the Lord said, "*I am Jesus whom you are persecuting. But rise and stand upon your feet; for I have appeared to you for this purpose, to appoint you to serve and bear witness to the things in which you have seen me and to those in which I will appear to you delivering you from the people and from the Gentiles-to whom I send you to open their eyes, that they may turn from darkness to light and from the power of Satan to God, that they may receive forgiveness of sin and a place among those who are sanctified by faith in me.*" (Acts 20:15-18).

He felt himself bound to serve

"He wrote, *I am under obligation both to Greeks and to barbarians, both to the wise and to the foolish: I am eager to preach the gospel to you who are in Rome.*" (Romans 1:14-15).

"For necessity is laid upon me. Woe is me if I do not preach the gospel." (I Corinthians 9:16).

"Thus making it my ambition to preach the gospel, not where Christ has already been named, lest I build on another man's foundation." (Romans 15:20).

HE PAID THE PRICE THAT WAS NEEDED

"I pommel my body and subdue it, lest after preaching to others I myself should be disqualified." (I Corinthians 9:27).

"For though I am free from all men, I have made myself a slave to all, that I might win the more. To the Jews I became as a Jew, in order to win the Jews..." (I Corinthians 9:19-20).

"Just as I try to please all men in every thing I do, not seeking my own advantage but that of many, that they may be saved." (I Corinthians 10:33).

"On the contrary, I worked harder than any of them, though it was not I but the grace of God which is in me." (I Corinthians 15:10).

"I coveted no one's silver or gold or apparel. You yourselves know that these hands ministered to my necessities, and to those who were with me. In all things I have shown you that by so toiling one must help the weak, remembering the words of the Lord Jesus, how he said, "It is more blessed to give than to receive." (Acts 20:33-35).

"To the present hour, we hunger and thirst, we are ill-clad and buffeted and homeless, and we labour, working with our own hands..." (I Corinthians 4:11-12).

"For you remember our labour and toil, brethren; for we worked night and day, that we might not burden any of you, while we preached to you the gospel of God." (I Thessalonians 2:9).

Paul had a goal and accomplished it

"But I do not account my life of any value nor as precious to myself, if only I may accomplish my course and the ministry which I received from the Lord Jesus, to testify to the gospel of the grace of God." (Acts 20:24).

"I am already on the point of being sacrificed; the time of my departure has come. I have fought a good fight, I have finished the race, I have kept the faith. Henceforth there is laid up for me the crown of righteousness, which the Lord, the righteous judge will award to me on that day, and not only to me but also to all who have loved his appearing" (II Timothy 4:6-8).

He accomplished it through great and utter exertion

"Not that I have already obtained this or am already perfect; but I press on to make it my own. Brethren, I do not consider that I have made it my own, but one thing I do, forgetting what lies behind and straining forward to what lies ahead, I press on toward the goal for the prize of the upward call of God in Christ Jesus." (Philippians 3:13-14).

"Him we proclaim, warning every man and teaching every man in all wisdom, that we may present every man mature in Christ. For this I toil, striving with all the energy which he mightily inspires within me. For I want you to know how I strive for you, and for those at

Laodicea, and for all who have not seen my face." (Colossians 1:28-2:1).

HE USED WORDS AND PHRASES WHICH ALL WHO WORK HARD CANNOT RUN AWAY FROM IN THEIR EXPERIENCE.

1. I am under obligation
2. I am eager
3. Necessity is laid on me
4. Woe is me if I preach not the gospel
5. Thus making it my ambition
6. I pommel my body.
7. I subdue my body.
8. I have made myself a slave to all.
9. I try to please all men in all I do, not seeking my own advantage but that of many so that they may be saved.
10. I coveted no one's silver or gold or apparel.
11. These hands ministered to my necessities and to those who were with me.
12. By so toiling, one must help the weak.
13. We hunger and thirst.
14. We labour, working with our own hands.
15. Our labour and toil
16. We worked night and day.
17. I do not account my life of any value.
18. If only I may accomplish my course and the ministry I received.
19. I have fought a good fight
20. I have finished the race

21. I have kept the faith.
22. There is laid up for me.
23. I press on.
24. One thing I do
25. Straining forward
26. Pressing on toward the goal
27. I toil, striving with all the energy
28. I strive for you.

THEREFORE

Anyone who is not prepared to pommel his body and subdue it, who is not prepared to labour, toil, work night and day, press on, strain, etc. is not working hard. He will certainly not accomplish the call of God on his life.

PAUL SUCCEEDED

The apostle Paul succeeded. He planted churches, led many to the Lord, trained them and is reaching many people for the Lord even today through the epistles he wrote.

At the beginning of his walk with God it was said to him, "You will be a witness for him to all men of what you have seen and heard". He is today being a witness. Until the gospel of the Kingdom has been published to every nation as a witness, Paul will still be at work. He worked. He is working and he will work. This is because of how hard and how faithful he was while he was here.

May you go and do likewise! Amen.

2

C. T. STUDD and hard work.

C.T. Studd was one of the most outstanding missionaries who ever lived. He was a famous cricketer who turned his back to fame and became a missionary to China. Later on he gave away all of his enormous fortune to the service of the Lord. He next served the Lord in India and at the age of fifty-three, he left for pioneering work in Africa at the call of the Lord whom he loved. He served in Africa for about eighteen years without ever returning home to Britain until the Lord called him home at about the age of seventy. His entire life was one of sacrifice and hard work. He sacrificed fame and position in the world, sacrificed his fortune, sacrificed his family (he was separated from his wife for almost his entire stay in Africa) and laboured as few people ever did.

CT STUDD WAS DISCIPLINED

of him it was said, "Charlie was one of those boys who goes all out for the thing he loves. He was tremendously keen on cricket, and he was determined to do well at it. Upstairs in his bedroom at home there was a big wardrobe with a long glass. In front of it was a seam down the centre. The way he argued to himself was this: If a man puts a dead straight bat every time in front of the ball, it must be impossible for the ball to hit the wicket. So he made it his first business to learn to play with a straight bat. Hour after hour he practised in front of the looking glass, keeping his bat along the seam of the carpet. He used to be ragged for taking things so seriously, but he stuck to it.

Another dodge of his a little later on was to make sure that he had his eye in for the first ball he had to play. If he was the next man, he would sit on the edge of the ground with his eyes glued to a spot on the grass about 22 yards in front, so as to have his eye exactly accustomed to the length of the pitch from the moment he was at the wicket. He never smoked and would not even remain in the dining room after dinner, lest the smoke should affect his eye.

Because of such discipline, his biographer wrote, "Though only a third-year man at the University, he rose to the very top of the cricket world, amateur and professional alike. It is doubtful whether any other undergraduate in the history of cricket has done such a thing."

CT STUDD WORKED HARD IN GIVING AWAY HIS FORTUNE

"One day (he writes) when I was reading the harmony of the Gospels, I came to where Christ talked with the rich young man. Then God seemed to bring back to me all the vows I had made. A few days later, the post which only came every half month, brought letters from the solicitor and banker to tell me what I had inherited. Then God made me just ordinarily honest and told me what to do. Then I learnt why I had been sent to Chungking. I needed to draw up papers granting the power of attorney and for that I had to have the signature of one of Her Majesty's officers. I went to the Consul, but when he saw the paper, he said, 'I won't sign it.' Finally, he said he would give me two weeks to think it over, and then if I still wished it, he would sign. At the end of two weeks, I took it back to him and he signed it and off the stuff went. God has promised to give an hundred fold for everything we give Him. An hundredfold is a wonderful percentage; it is 10.000 per cent."

So far as he could judge, his inheritance was 29.000 pounds; But in order to leave a margin for error, he decided to start by giving 25.000 pounds. One memorable day, January 13, 1887, he sent off four cheques of 5000 pounds each, and five of 1.000 pounds. As coolly and deliberately as a businessman invests in some "gilt edged" securities, as being both safe and yield good interest, so C.T. invested in the bank of Heaven."

CT STUDD FOUNDED HIS WORLD EVANGELIZATION CRUSADE ON A SUPREME SACRIFICE, DETERMINATION AND COURAGE

He wrote, "Our method is to search and find out what parts of the world at present remain unevangelized, and then by faith in Christ, by prayer to God, by obedience to the Holy Spirit, by courage, determination, and supreme sacrifice, to accomplish their evangelization with utmost dispatch."

Do you notice what he deemed necessary?

1. Faith in Christ

2. Prayer to God
3. Obedience to the Holy Spirit
4. Courage
5. Determination
6. Supreme sacrifice,

The last three: Courage, determination, and supreme sacrifice are indispensable ingredients for hard work. His philosophy was, "If Jesus Christ be God and died for me, then no sacrifice can be too great for me to make for Him."

CT STUDD MAINTAINED A SPIRIT OF EXACTITUDE IN ALL THINGS

"He was particular to the last detail in such tasks as these (building). Every pole had to be exactly the right length placed in the right angle, etc; and he had a purpose in it, for the natives must be taught that good Christianity and lazy or bad workmanship are utter contradictions. He believed that one of the best ways to teach a native that righteousness is the foundation of God's Throne was by making him see that absolute straightness and accuracy is the only law of success in material things. He put the same concentration and the same determination to do the best into matters of minor importance such as these, as into his preaching or cricket of early years. If he had a building job on, and it had arrived at the stage in which it needed careful supervision, it was hopeless to wait for him for breakfast. It was 10 a.m., mid-day, and sometimes even 3 and 4 p.m. before he would stop to have food. I have seen him set one of his small boys to search a whole day for one button which the boy had lost, not because of the prized button, but to teach the boy thoroughness and carefulness."

CT STUDD PUT IN LONG HOURS

He was a sickly man all his life. "He was a museum of diseases when he left China, and was afterwards hardly ever free. He had "asthma, recurring malaria and dysentery and the chills and pains of gallstones ever with him in varying combination." However, "He was able to go on working not 8 but 18 hours a day, addressing, often for hours, thousands of his fellow creatures, telling them of Jesus Christ and the wonders of His love--and this, to the very end of his days. He was one the finest Christians and the most heroic and lovable man I ever met."

He woke regularly between 2.30 a.m. and 3.00 and never went to bed until he had finished his evening meetings which went from 7 p.m. to 10 p.m.

Towards the end of his life, it was said of him, "In spite of the enormous amount of work he was already doing, he determined to translate the New Testament into Kingwana. It was a marvellous intellectual feat for a man of nearly seventy, quite apart from the weeks of extra-work involved. He worked at it night and day. 'My days,' he wrote, 'are eighteen hours as a rule, and no meals but what I gulp down as I write.' Much of it was done in the early morning between 2 a.m. and 6 a.m."

(From C.T. STUDD by Norman Grubb, C.L.C Fort Washington, Pennsylvania, U.S.A.).

Is there any question in your heart that he worked hard ?

3

Gideon and hard work.

There was a period when the children of Israel sinned and the Lord gave them into the hand of Midian for seven years. The people of Israel were brought very low because of the Midianites and they cried to the Lord for help. The Lord decided to set them free. He went out in search of a man who could be used as a deliverer. God is the Eternal Deliverer, but in His sovereignty, He has ordained that He will not move to deliver until He finds a human being through whom He will carry out His acts of deliverance. He is looking for human deliverers. In the case at hand, God went out in search of a human being who could be used by the Eternal Deliverer as the human deliverer. The Bible says, "*Now, the angel of the Lord came and sat under the oak at Ophrah, which belonged to Joash the Abiezrite, as his son Gideon was beating out wheat in the wine press, to hide it from the Midianites. And the angel of the Lord appeared to him and said, "The Lord is with you, you mighty man of valour... And the Lord turned to him and said, "Go in this might of yours and deliver Israel from the hand of Midian; Do not I send you ?' And he said to him, 'Pray, Lord, how can I deliver Israel ? Behold, my clan is the weakest in Manasseh, and I am the least in my family.' And the Lord said to him, 'But I will be with you, and you shall smite the Midianites as one man.*" (Judges 6:11-16).

GIDEON BEFORE THE CALL OF GOD

There were many young men in Israel at the time when God called Gideon. Why did He choose Gideon ? Was it a random choice ? Certainly not. God does not choose people at random. He chooses people on the basis of what they already are before the call and what they will be after the call.

Gideon had one thing that is indispensable for all whom the Lord calls to responsibility. He had a hard-working spirit and was putting himself to work. This is immediately obvious from the Lord's words to him, and what he was doing when the Lord called him.

He was beating out wheat in the wine press to hide it from the Midianites. He was at work. He was busy. He was working hard. He was working in a goal-directed way. He was totally involved in productivity. In the process, he had become a man of valour in the Lord's estimation. For the Lord to esteem him a man of valour means that he had indeed worked hard, not just for that day, but for all his life. It is likely that he had worked hard before Israel was subjected by the Midianites and continued to work very hard after Israel was subdued. GOD IS LOOKING FOR PEOPLE WHO HAVE MASTERED THE ART OF HARD WORK BE IT IN BEATING WHEAT, SWEEPING FLOORS, CUTTING GRASS, SELLING IN A STORE, WORKING HARD IN AN OFFICE AND SO ON, TO COMMISSION FOR OTHER AND "HIGHER" SERVICES IN HIS VINEYARD TODAY.

Had Gideon not built such a history, God would not have chosen him to become a co-deliverer with Him. Had Gideon not built such a history, God would not have found what He was looking for--a hard-working man. When we look at

Scripture and history, we see very clearly that those whom God called and used in a singular way were people who were all working hard at something before they received the special call of God. Let us look at a few examples to clarify the point.

Moses was mighty in word and deed before he was called for royal service in God's University of Midian where he specialized in keeping the flock. The Bible says, "*And Moses was instructed in all the wisdom of the Egyptians, and he was mighty in his words and deeds.*" (Acts 7:22). He unquestionably worked hard.

David, before he was appointed King in private by the prophet Samuel, had also spent many years in the University of the Hills mastering the rare art of keeping the flock. He too was on the special honours roll there. He presented his credentials to King Saul in the following terms: "*Your servant used to keep sheep for his father; and when there came a lion, or bear, and took a lamb from the flock, I went after him and smote him and delivered it out of his mouth; and if he arose against me, I caught him by his beard, and smote him and killed him. Your servant has killed both lions and bears; and this uncircumcised Philistine shall be like one of them seeing he has defied the armies of the living God.*" (I Samuel 17:34-36). Others testified of him saying, "*Behold I have seen a son of Jesse the Bethlehemite, who is skilful in playing, a man of valour, a man of war, prudent in speech, a man of good presence; and the Lord is with him.*" (I Samuel 16:18).

Saul of Tarsus, before he became Paul, was not idle. He had laboured hard and was totally taken up by what was then the goal of his life. His own testimony of it is, "*Though I have reason for confidence in the flesh also. If any other man thinks he has reason for confidence in the flesh, I have more...as to the law a Pharisee, as to zeal, a persecutor of the church, as to righteousness under the law blameless."* (Philippians 3:4-6). *"I myself was convinced that I ought to do many things in opposing the name of Jesus of Nazareth. And I did so in Jerusalem. I not only shut up many of the saints in prison, by authority from the chief priests, but when they were put to death, I cast my vote against them. And I punished them often in all the synagogues, and tried to make them blaspheme; and in raging fury against them, I persecuted them even to foreign cities."*(Acts 16:9-11). Of him it was said, *"But Saul, still breathing threats and murder against the disciples of the Lord, went to the high priest and asked him for letters to the synagogue at Damascus, so that if he found any belonging to the way, men or women, he might bring them bound to Jerusalem."* (Acts 9:1-2). He unquestionably worked hard.

C.T. Studd unquestionably worked hard to become a foremost cricketer before the call of God took him to China, India and finally to Africa.

John Sung unquestionably worked hard, earned a Bachelor's degree in three years, a master's degree in 9 months and a Doctorate's degree in 19 months, being honoured among the four top-most students in all American universities, reading the Bible forty times in six months before he became aflame for God all over China.

Gideon at the call of God

It can be said that the call of God is preceded by the call of man. Those who have faithfully attended to the call of man will receive the call of God. Gideon had answered the call of man to beat wheat in the wine press in order to hide it from the Midianites. He was right at it, faithfully doing it with all his heart, putting all of himself into it when God called him to deliver His people. God's call comes to people at work. It comes to people in active service. It comes to people who have worked hard and who are working hard. Those who worked hard in the past but have retired from working hard and given themselves to laziness and idleness are exempted from further service. It is not enough to start well. One must continue to work hard.

Gideon continued to work hard. His might was current. He was told, "Go in this might of yours and deliver Israel from the hand of Midian." It was 'this might of yours'--present might.

David was called from keeping sheep to be anointed king. In fact, he was anointed the same day that he came from the place where he had been busily keeping the flock, killing lions and bears in their defence and learning the art of being a musician of note and a writer.

Saul of Tarsus was arrested on his way working hard against the Church.

Moses was actively keeping sheep when he turned to see the burning bush and then the call of God came.

Barnabas and Saul were actively worshipping the Lord with fasting when the word of the Lord asked that they be set aside for apostolic duties.

THE HERE AND THE NOW IS IMPORTANT -- THE THING YOU ARE INVOLVED IN YEAR BY YEAR, MONTH BY MONTH AND SECOND BY SECOND. BEWARE OF THAT SECOND BEING SPENT IN IDLENESS. IT COULD COST YOU TOO MUCH!

GIDEON WORKED HARD AFTER THE CALL

many people have lost out with God because they considered the call of God as the height of glory and not a position for service. Gideon was different.

First of all, he worked hard in explaining to God that he was not able. He was humble. He was far from presumptuous. He brought out that which disqualified him:

1. My clan is the weakest in Manasseh.
2. I am the least in my family.

He was qualified, but he was not self assuming. He did not elevate himself. He could really serve the Lord and His purposes.

Secondly, he worked hard in receiving assurance from the Lord.

Thirdly, he worked hard at destroying the altar of Baal.

Fourthly, he worked hard at recruiting an army.

Fifthly, he worked hard at surrendering to God and believing God that a small army of overcomers was better than multitudes of people who were overcome by fear or divided at heart.

Sixthly, he worked hard at attacking the enemy, crushing him and pressing on even though faint until there was complete victory.

Lastly, he worked hard to stay out of being made a ruler, a fact that shows that his interest was solely obedience to the Lord and nothing else. The Bible says, "*Then the men of Israel said to Gideon, Rule over us, you and your son and your grandson also; for you have delivered us out of the hand of Midian. Gideon said to them, I will not rule over you; the Lord will rule over you."* (Judges 8:22-23). He served and refused to enjoy the fruit of it. He served and remained a servant. He served, won a great victory but did not become big in his own eyes. He served but saw himself only as a man used by the Lord. That is the spirit in which all who would work hard for the Lord must be. To serve, do great things for the Lord and not become taken up with self is one of the greatest things that can happen to a hard-working man. It happened to Gideon by his own choice. May it happen to you and to me! Amen.

4

Anna the prophetess and hard work.

Prayer is work. Prayer is very hard work. prayer is the hardest work that anyone could ever engage in on this side of heaven. The Lord Jesus was involved in working extremely hard all His life. However, it is in the realm of prayer that the total force of His All-glorious personality was poured out.

In the Garden of Gethsemane He prayed, "*Father, if thou art willing, remove this cup from me; nevertheless, not my will but thine be done.*" (Luke 22:42). So mighty was the exertion in prayer that it led to sweat drops of blood. The Bible says, "*And being in agony, he prayed more earnestly; and his sweat became like droplets of blood falling upon the ground.*" (Luke 22:44).

From the cross, He did not utter a simple prayer. Prayer became a loud cry, "*Eli, Eli, lama sabachthani*" *which is "My God, my God, why hast thou forsaken me?*" (Matthew 27:46).

The writer to the Hebrews wrote, "*In the days of his flesh, Jesus offered up prayers and supplications, with loud cries and tears, to him who was able to save him from death, and he was heard for his Godly fear.*" (Hebrews 5:7). So, prayer for the Lord Jesus was extreme hard work.

The apostle Paul commands, "*Pray at all times in the Spirit, with all prayer and supplication. To that end, keep alert in all perseverance, making supplication for all the saints, and also for me, that utterance may be given me in opening my mouth boldly to proclaim the mystery of the gospel.*" (Ephesians 6:18-19). He appealed to the Romans to strive with him in prayer. "*I appeal to you, brethren, by our Lord Jesus Christ and by the love of the Spirit, to strive together with me in your prayers to God on my behalf.*" (Romans 15:30). He was striving, labouring, toiling, pressing on with all his might and with all the strength which the Lord mightily inspired within him; and from that continuing experience, he was inviting the saints to join him.

It is with this background that we are brought face to face with one who worked extremely hard at prayer--the prophetess Anna.

HER VISION

Anna knew that there were many things being done for the Lord. She knew that what was being done was important. However, she knew that all that was being done would not succeed without prayer. She saw the indispensability of prayer. She knew that there were some things that God had decided would not happen unless man cooperated with Him in prayer. She knew that the devil was not bothered about any work against his kingdom which was not conceived in prayer and was not being carried out in dependence on God by calling Him in prayer. She knew that prayer was where the action really was. She also knew that there were very few people who were making prayer a priority. It dawned upon her that that was where God wanted her to invest her life.

Beyond that, she saw something that was even more important. The Saviour was expected but had not yet come. Her heart longed and burned for Him and she desired Him to come. So, she decided that she would invest her whole life into co-operating with God to ensure that the Messiah was born. She probably was allowed the privilege of seeing the angelic conflicts that were on as the enemy warred to prevent the Saviour from coming into the world. She decided to co-operate by fasting and praying.

Her labours

The Bible says, "*And there was a prophetess, Anna, the daughter of Phanuel, of the tribe of Asher; she was of a great age, having lived with her husband seven years from her virginity, and as a widow till she was eighty-four. She did not depart from the temple, worshipping with fasting and prayer night and day. And coming up at that very hour, she gave thanks to God, and spoke of him to all who were looking for the redemption of Jerusalem.*" (Luke 2:36-38).

Anna, perhaps, got married at 16. It would mean that at twenty-three, she was widowed. If she started her ministry at twenty-four, then by the time that the Messiah arrived in the temple she had been labouring at it for about sixty years.

Can you imagine her fasting for His return and praying for it for one year? Can you imagine that she went on for:

- five years
- ten years
- twenty years
- thirty years?

After thirty years of fasting and praying night and day, she had not given up. She was older but her faith made her continue. She put every minute into it -- night and day. She never went on holidays. She refused to be :

- tired
- weary
- discouraged
- side-tracked.

She focused on her goal. Like her forefather Abraham, "She grew strong in her faith as she gave glory to God." Then she went on until she had been fasting and praying night and day for:

- forty years
- fifty years
- sixty years.

She went grey in the process of waiting, worshipping, fasting and praying for sixty years !

She was not attracted or distracted by what was happening around. She had grown numb to all the joys and sorrows all around. She had only one desire--the Messiah, and for His coming she laboured night and day.

Think of it--she did not depart from the temple for about sixty years. She made herself a prisoner in the temple. She sacrificed all else and separated herself from all else and gave herself to just one thing--praying that the Saviour would come.

Then, one day He was there, right in the temple! She came up at that very hour during which He was in the temple. She gave thanks to God. She spoke of Him to those who were around, and then, she withdrew.

Her goal was accomplished. She had fought a good fight. She had kept the faith. She had finished her course. She had satisfied the heart of God. Amen !

ANYONE WHO LABOURS AT HIS GOAL AS SHE DID FOR HERS MUST SUCCEED. FOR SUCH, FAILURE IS IMPOSSIBLE. YOU, GO AND DO LIKEWISE.

In following her example, you will only be doing what our hard-working Jesus has been doing for over 1950 years. The Bible says, "***He always lives to make intercession for them.***" (Hebrews 7:25).

Prayer, real prayer, is very, very hard work. It is extreme hard work. Dare to be involved in it.

Amen.

In concluding

1

Working hard as a way of life.

It is possible to work hard at major projects but not work hard in the daily routine of life. This is bad. God works hard always.

There will be the major task to which God calls a man. There will be other tasks that God will give him along life's way. It is important that the small tasks be accomplished with diligence. The one who is faithful in little things will be faithful in big things, and the one who is faithful in small things will be given greater things to do. The one who is faithfully working for another will be given that which is his own. The Bible says, "*He who is faithful in a very little is faithful also in much; and he who is dishonest in a very little is dishonest also in much. If then you have not been faithful in the unrighteous mammon, who will entrust to you the true riches ? And if you have not been faithful in that which is another's, who will give you that which is your own?*" (Luke 16:10-12).

What does this mean? It means that you must make up your mind that you will put all of yourself into everything you do and labour at it with all your might.

You will bear in mind that God's examination for promotion is going on continuously and not just when big projects are concerned. This means that:

1. You will begin to walk fast and stop dragging yourself about lazily.
2. You will jump out of bed and not take ten minutes to be up.
3. You will run, if need be, and not walk leisurely if you are late.
4. Etc.

It also means that

1. If you are washing plates, you will work hard at them and save time.
2. If you are washing clothes, you will do the same.
3. If you are

- bathing,
- combing your hair,
- dressing,
- talking,
- writing a letter,
- thinking,
- answering a question,
- asking a question,
- making a suggestion,
- opening the door of a car,
- serving food,
- cooking food,

- eating food,
- serving water,
- drinking water,
- making a phone call,
- receiving a phone call,
- reading,
- walking,
- running,
- packing,
- encouraging someone,
- rebuking someone,
- working on a farm,
- etc,

you will put all of yourself into it and apply all of yourself at it and keep at it until the task is done.

The secret of it is to decide that if you are going to do anything, that thing must be important to God. (Never do anything that you do not consider important to the Lord). Therefore, if the thing is important to God, then it deserves all of your strength regardless of how small you think it is. If therefore, you are doing something for God, can you give it anything less than your

- total energy,
- total concentration,
- total being ?

Certainly not; You will surely put all of yourself in if you know that you are doing it for Him.

You have been bought by Him. You are doubly His: first of all, by right of His being your Creator and secondly, by right of His being your Redeemer. All you do is for Him and anything that you cannot do for Him should not be done at all.

- What I mean is that unless your
- bathing,
- combing of hair,
- dressing,
- talking,
- writing a letter,
- thinking,
- answering a question,
- etc

is for His honour and glory, it should not be done at all. Unless these things directly or indirectly contribute to the building of His kingdom, they should not be done.

If on the other hand, they are a part of the building of His kingdom, then you should give them all of your strength, and all of yourself as you would give them to Him were you is in His presence now. Actually, you are indeed in His presence. He is seeing all that you do and He is assessing the way you are giving yourself to it.

Decide that you will not do something in two minutes that you can do in one minute if you exert yourself. Always exert all of yourself in anything you do and thereby save time for the next thing. Never give anyone a cold handshake. Put all of yourself into it. Shake that hand as you would shake God's hand were He to stretch it out to you. Wash those plates as fast as possible and as thoroughly as possible as if the Lord were waiting to be served and you were going to serve Him in them.

Decide that you will not hold yourself back from anything in which you are involved. Give all of yourself away. If you are talking to someone, give him 100% attention. Forget about everyone else and everything else. Pour yourself out and satisfy that person. When you have finished with one thing or one situation, forget it completely and prepare for the next. Do not attend to the next person with thoughts of the last person you related to clouding your mind. Make every new contact the most important of your life for that moment, and when it is over, move to the next and do the same.

As you work hard in every situation, you will develop the right habits and the right attitudes to

- time
- people
- things
- energy
- etc

and these will be applicable in all situations and thus make you a success ! Amen.

2

The importance of faithfulness.

We have talked about working hard and this has to be. However, we recognize that there are some positions where the Lord may place His own in which their work cannot be assessed in the terms that we have written about. Their work can be assessed in terms of faithfulness or unfaithfulness.

Take for example, a servant who waits on a master at table. All that is required of him is that he be clean, well-mannered, and available at table, waiting to do whatever he is told to do. If it is required that he so waits twenty-four hours each day for sixty years, then all he can do is to be:

- clean
- available
- alert
- obedient

for all those years and he will obtain top marks from the Lord for working hard.

Take another example of a servant whose duty is to protect his master from the enemy. All he has to do to obtain top marks from his heavenly Master is to be at his duty post at the said times and be fully alert to ensure that the enemy does not come in and destroy the master. He has to be there at the right time and he has to watch so that the master is safe.

- He shall not slumber.
- He shall not sleep.
- He shall not be distracted.

He shall concentrate throughout because he does not know when the enemy might come. He is well aware that if he is inattentive at any one moment, that could be the time during which the enemy chooses to come in, and the harm done would be terrible beyond telling. Therefore, to be alert throughout and prepared to fight to protect the master becomes the goal of his life. He labours to be alert, to concentrate and to fight to defend the master in case of attack.

Another example that may be given is that of an armour-bearer. He is not the fighter. All he has to do is to be the armour-bearer. He has to be faithful. He has to keep close to the fighting captain. He has to ensure that the armour is available and it is ready. He has no other ambitions. He has no other projects. He has no other goals. All these have already been decided for him. All he has to do is to be where the captain is and hold the armour at his disposal. He must concentrate. He must take risks. He must just follow the captain. If the captain is attacked, he is attacked. He has his eye fixed on the captain and any moment when the hand is stretched for the armour, it must be placed in his hand immediately.

One hymn-writer wrote:

"Surely, my Captain may depend on me even though I may be only an armour-bearer."

Yes, not a fighter but an armour-bearer! However, there may come a day when the battle is decided, not by the skills of the captain, but by the faithfulness of the armour-bearer! Can you imagine a situation in which the captain penetrates the territory of the enemy on the assumption that his armour-bearer is following close at hand and when it is time to strike the enemy, he sends out his hand for the armour and none is put into his hand,and on turning to look, he does not see the armour-bearer because he had been distracted by someone or by something ? Well, the enemy will kill the captain and win the war and the battle will have been decided, not by the skill of the captain, but by the unfaithfulness of the armour-bearer.

God has not called many of us to plan and execute great schemes for Him. He has called a few to such responsibilities and the vast majority of us to be

- armour-bearers;
- watchmen
- servants
- helpers

of those He has placed in authority, and our rank in heaven will be determined by whether or not we were faithful.

God expects faithfulness from the captain in that capacity.

God expects faithfulness from the servant in that capacity.

The faithful captain will receive a full reward.

The faithful servant will receive a full reward.

The unfaithful captain will be disqualified.

The unfaithful servant will be disqualified.

The servant or armour-bearer who, instead of serving in that capacity, invents a project of his own and sacrifices all that he is and all that he has to do it, thereby hoping to please the heavenly Captain, will be disqualified because he has done that which he desired and not that which the Lord assigned to him. All must receive their assignments from their heavenly Captain, be it to be earthly captains, or servants of earthly captains whom they serve as unto the heavenly Captain.

The Lord looks first of all to see if a person is where He placed him. It is only those who have laboured at the place where He placed them who can be evaluated as to the quality and quantity of their labours. All the others are disqualified regardless of what they sacrificed and how much they achieved.

THERE IS NO SUBSTITUTE FOR FAITHFULNESS

the Lord has called His not to be great but to be faithful. In His Word, He says the following about faithfulness and the faithful:

1. *"Who then is the faithful and wise servant, whom his master has set over his household, to give them their food at the proper time? Blessed is that servant whom his master when he comes will find so doing."* (Matthew 24:45-46).
2. *"Well done, good and faithful servant; you have been faithful over a little, I will set you over much; enter into the joy of your master."* (Matthew 25:21).

3. *"He who is faithful in a very little is faithful also in much; and he who is dishonest in a very little is dishonest also in much."* (Luke 16:10).
4. *"If then you have not been faithful in the unrighteous mammon, who will entrust to you the true riches* ?" (Luke 16:11).
5. *"And if you have not been faithful in that which is another's, who will give you that which is your own* ?" (Luke 16:12).

What is faithfulness ?

1. The question may arise in some heart, "What is faithfulness?" We reply that faithfulness is being all that the Lord expects you to be, doing what he has given you at the time and place of His instruction for His glory and in doing it, putting in all that you are and all that you have, holding nothing back.

Faithfully working hard serving man?

there are many who say that they want to serve God directly and do not want to serve man. This is pride which is an abomination before God. In addition, it is great ignorance. There is hardly anything that anyone can do for God without doing it for man.

The Lord Jesus was a Servant of man. He served very ordinary people. He served lepers, prostitutes, etc.

The apostles served and serve men, even lost men.

Prophets, evangelists, pastors, teachers and all who are involved in serving the Lord do this by serving man. There is no way out. Even those who intercede serve man; for they intercede for man.

So, if you have an opportunity to serve some servant of God, count it as a great privilege and do it faithfully as you would do if you were serving Jesus. The Bible says, "*Whatever your task, work heartily, as serving the Lord and not men, knowing that from the Lord you will receive the inheritance as your reward; you are serving the Lord Christ.*" (Colossians 3:23). The Lord Jesus said, "*Then they also will answer, Lord, when did we see thee hungry or thirsty or a stranger or naked or sick or in prison, and did not minister to thee ? Then he will answer them, Truly, I say to you, as you did it not to one of the least of these, you did it not to me.*" (Matthew 25:44-45).

There is also the matter of rewards. The best rewards will go to those who are slaves of men and the second best to those who are servants of men. Anyone who is a boss on earth will have no rank in heaven; for only slaves and servants will have ranks there. The Lord Jesus taught saying, "*You know that those who are supposed to rule over the Gentiles lord it over them, and their great men exercise authority over them. But it shall not be so among you; but whosoever would be great among you must be your servant, and whoever would be first among you must be the slave of all. For the Son of man also came not to be served but to serve, and to give his life as a ransom for many.*" (Mark 10:42-45).

So, if you want to be great, be a servant of all in spirit and the Lord may decide that you should be the servant of one person in particular. If, on the other hand, you are not content to be only great but desire ardently to be first, decide and be the slave of all in general and the Lord may appoint you to be the slave of one of the slaves of men. Then you will be first in heaven !

Think about it and do something about it! Do it faithfully:

- every day,
- every hour,
- every minute,
- every second !

3

Rejoicing at work.

It is possible to work for the Lord grumbling. It is sad; for such have not seen. Those who have seen consider it a privilege to do even the slightest service for Him, either directly in praise and adoration or indirectly in serving Him through serving man. The apostle exhorts, "*Do all things without grumbling or questioning, that you may be blameless and innocent, children of God without blemish in the midst of a crooked and perverse generation, among whom you shine as lights in the world.*" (Philippians 2:14-15).

You are not only not to grumble. You are not to be resigned to working hard for the Lord as if you were doomed to do it.

You are to rejoice for the privilege of serving Him by working hard. The Bible says, "*Rejoice in the Lord always; again I will say, Rejoice.*" (Philippians 4:4). "*Give thanks in all circumstances; for this is the will of God in Christ Jesus for you.*" (I Thessalonians 5:18). "*Continue steadfastly in prayer, being watchful in it with thanksgiving.*" (Colossians 4:2).

The apostle Paul rejoiced in the privilege of working for the Lord even when that privilege was working for the Lord through suffering. He wrote, "*More than that, we rejoice in our sufferings, knowing that suffering produces endurance."* (Romans 5:3). Do you remember that when they were locked up unjustly at Philippi, at midnight they were praying and singing hymns to God, and the prisoners were listening to them. (Acts 16:25). Please, remember to do the following:

1. Start your work rejoicing.
2. Continue to rejoice as you work.
3. Stop and thank the Lord for every step of the work that has been completed.
4. Stop and sing a song of praise to the Lord at each step completed.
5. Rejoice and praise the Lord as you begin the next step.
6. Praise the Lord as you face an obstacle and rejoice in Him.
7. Praise the Lord as you labour to take away the obstacle.
8. Praise the Lord with rejoicing as the obstacle is removed.
9. Praise and rejoice in the Lord at the beginning of every new day of work.
10. Praise and rejoice in the Lord at the end of every day of work.
11. Rejoice in the Lord at the end of the project.
12. Hold a feast of rejoicing and thanksgiving to celebrate the end of the project.
13. Rejoice as you pray about the next project.
14. Rejoice as you start it.
15. Rejoice every day.
16. Rejoice always.
17. Rejoice now.

18. As much as possible, sing a song of rejoicing and thanksgiving to the Lord.
19. Praise the Lord!

4

Resting from what ?

The Bible tells us that when God finished His work, He rested. He did not rest before the work was finished. He rested after He had finished the work, inspected it and passed the verdict that it was very good. The Bible puts it this way, "*Thus the heavens and the earth were finished, and all the host of them. And on the seventh day, God finished his work which he had done and he rested on the seventh day from all his work which he had done.*" (Genesis 2:1-2).

It is obvious that no believer can afford to go on holiday on this side of heaven. War is in progress. Although the enemy was destroyed on the cross by the Lord Jesus, he was not annihilated. He has limited powers and is doing his worst even now. The apostle Paul wrote, "*Put on the whole armour of God, that you may be able to stand against the wiles of the devil. For we are not contending against flesh and blood, but against the principalities, against the powers, against the world rulers of this present darkness, against the spiritual hosts of wickedness in the heavenly places. Therefore take the whole armour of God, that you may be able to stand in the evil day, and having done all, to stand. Stand therefore, having girded your loins with truth, and having put on the breastplate of righteousness, and having shod your feet with the equipment of the gospel of peace; besides all these, take the shield of faith with which you can quench all the flaming darts of the evil one. And take the helmet of salvation, and the sword of the Spirit, which is the word of God.* (Ephesians 6:11-17).

Can you imagine a soldier dressed as above who decides to take

- one week
- two weeks
- three weeks

and go to another

- country
- state
- part of the country to
- relax,
- swim,
- hunt,
- play tennis
  golf
  . etc ?

I cannot understand it, but it is being done today by many hirelings who pose as "shepherds of the sheep of the Most High God". They are not shepherds. They are hirelings. Only hirelings can abandon the sheep and go away for a week or more to relax and enjoy the passing pleasures of a judged world. I know a man of God who laboured for at least fourteen hours each day in various aspects of tending the Lord's flock who did not take one day's rest in forty years !

Let us look at it this way, is it accepted that officers, captains, colonels, generals and field marshals go on holiday when there is a fierce conflict ? It does not happen in worldly battles. Only mad people can practise it in the Battle of battles. The sad thing is that many people are resting from laziness. They spend the year doing very little and then go on holiday to rest from laziness. This is a shame. Such men and women should not be imitated. They are spies sent by the enemy to ruin the army of the Lord!

As for you, remember that you have no continuing city here. You seek the one to come. Keep at your work. Keep working hard. We recommend that you should work for 14-18 hours each day. Your eating and other things should occupy the 2-6 hours and you should sleep for not more than 4 hours. If you work that hard, you can ask the Lord to touch and refresh your body and you will be strong indefinitely. It will be good for a person who is working 18 or more hours a day to take one day in the week to rest and to concentrate on prayer and other things that help to deepen his knowledge of the Lord. The seventh day is the Lord's day-to be spent in His presence and for His glory.

We insist that the body can be disciplined to do any God-approved function. It can also be allowed through refusal to discipline, to become a tyrant that requires

1. 8-10 hours of sleep
2. 2-4 hours of idleness
3. large quantities of food.

This is not acceptable from a soldier of Christ.

When you have decided to give yourself 4 hours of rest every day, we recommend that you sleep for three hours at night and that the remaining hour be reserved for siesta or for short, quick naps of 5-10 minutes. For those who have their body systems under control, five minutes of sleep can have far-reaching healing and renewing effects.

I hear of people who lie down and for hours, they are not able to sleep. A few such cases may need medical attention, but for most of them, there is only one cure--hard work. They are trying to rest before they have worked hard and the body system is saying, "No sleep for the lazy."

We recommend that every night before you go to bed, you should take a note book and write what you want to rest from before you ask God to bless you and protect you while you sleep.

SLEEPING AS A ROUTINE

There are people who have developed a life style that is based on routine. They eat at particular hours regardless of whether or not they are hungry. They also sleep at particular hours, regardless of whether or not they have worked hard and as a result of that are tired and need rest. This ought not to be so. Never go to bed unless you have worked very hard and are tired and/or sleepy. To rest after doing nothing is sin! Do not commit sin in this way again.

5

The next project.

As we have said, the Lord keeps a person on earth primarily for the purpose of serving Him and thereby training the person to reign with Him in the Kingdom. This being so, there is no room whatsoever for anyone to be idle. The hymn-writer put it this way:

"Let none hear you idly saying

There is nothing I can do

While the souls of men are dying

And the Saviour calls for you

Take the task He gives you gladly

Let His work your pleasure be

Answer quickly when He calleth

Here I am send me, send me."

The Lord calls some people to a number of duties of which when one is finished, there is room for the next. C.T. Studd was called first to China, then to India and finally to Africa. He did not remain in China or in India beyond the time allotted to him by the Lord. He moved on at the command of the Lord. He was open to the Lord, ever wanting to know Him and serve Him with his whole might.

When he was nearly fifty-three years old and very sick, he did not settle down at home to wait for death. He was not tuned to diseases and symptoms. Rather, he was tuned to the voice of his Lord. At that advanced age and very sick, he desired only one thing - to serve the Lord with his whole might. That became his third and last project; for he went to the Congo, lived there for about seventeen years and died there, never even returning to Britain for a holiday. It was his third project, but it was also his greatest. It took hold of a whole region and contributed to giving birth to the World Evangelization Crusade which is active today in all the continents.

You may be nearing the end of your first project. You may be:

- thirty,
- forty,
- fifty,
- sixty,
- seventy,
- eighty,
- ninety.

Do not make death the next project. Look up to the Lord and ask Him, "Lord, what is the next goal you have for me?" Ask and ask. Do not make arrangements to die. Remember what the Hymn-writer wrote:

"But, Lord, 'tis for Thee, For Thy coming, we wait;

The sky, not the grave, is our goal:

Oh trump of the angel! Oh voice of the Lord!"

Blessed hope! Blessed rest of my soul.

Yes, echo with him saying, "The sky, not the grave is my goal." Look to the Lord. Look towards the sky. Be caught up with Him. The next project may be different, but it will demand all that the last project demanded and more. It will demand intense hard work in being close to Him in

- prayer
- intercession
- waiting upon Him
- working hard
- etc.

It will demand all the force that your

- spirit,
- soul,
- body,

are capable of. It will always demand your all, for it will be a project of the Lord who gave His all and demands our all. You will have all the force needed. You gave all your energy at:

- thirty and worked extremely hard
- forty and did the same
- fifty and did the same
- etc.

You will have all the energy required for the project that the Lord calls you to carry out for Him at ninety or a hundred.

The strength may not be equivalent to what you had in the past. However, that is not important. The important thing is that you will put in your all and you will hold nothing back. Do you remember the widow who put in two small coins into the treasury and was proclaimed by the Lord to have given more than those who put in: large sums? Do that. All that the Lord wanted in the past was your all. He has not changed. All that He wants today is your all:

- all your energy, even if you have to lie on a bed and pray.
- all your energy, even if all you can do is groan in prayer.
- all your energy, even if all you can do is to counsel straying people.

He wants all your energy. Give Him all and satisfy His heart and yours.

Very important

If you have not yet received Jesus as your Lord and Saviour, I encourage you to receive Him. Here are some steps to help you,

Admit that you are a sinner by nature and by practice and that on your own you are without hope. Tell God you have personally sinned against Him in your thoughts, words and deeds. Confess your sins to Him, one after another in a sincere prayer. Do not leave out any sins that you can remember. Truly turn from your sinful ways and abandon them. If you stole, steal no more. If you have been committing adultery or fornication, stop it. God will not forgive you if you have no desire to stop sinning in all areas of your life, but if you are sincere, He will give you the power to stop sinning.

Believe that Jesus Christ, who is God's Son, is the only Way, the only Truth and the only Life. Jesus said, «*I am the way, the truth and the life; no one comes to the Father, but by me*» (John 14:6). The Bible says, «*For there is one God, and there is one mediator between God and men, the man Christ Jesus, who gave himself as a ransom for all*» (1 Timothy 2:5-6). «*And there is salvation in no one else (apart from Jesus), for there is no other name under heaven given among men by which we must be saved*» (Acts 4:12). «*But to all who received him, who believed in his name, he gave power to become children of God...*» (John 1:12). But,

Consider the cost of following Him. Jesus said that all who follow Him must deny themselves, and this includes selfish financial, social and other interests. He also wants His followers to take up their crosses and follow Him. Are you prepared to abandon your own interests daily for those of Christ? Are you prepared to be led in a new direction by Him? Are you prepared to suffer for Him and die for Him if need be? Jesus will have nothing to do with half-hearted people. His demands are total. He will only receive and forgive those who are prepared to follow Him AT ANY COST. Think about it and count the cost. If you are prepared to follow Him, come what may, then there is something to do.

Invite Jesus to come into your heart and life. He says, *«Behold I stand at the door and knock. If anyone hears my voice and opens the door (to his heart and life), I will come in to him and eat with him, and he with me «* (Revelation 3:20). Why don't you pray a prayer like the following one or one of your own construction as the Holy Spirit leads ?

> «Lord Jesus, I am a wretched, lost sinner who has sinned in thought, word and deed. Forgive all my sins and cleanse me. Receive me, Saviour and transform me into a child of God. Come into my heart now and give me eternal life right now. I will follow you at all costs, trusting the Holy Spirit to give me all the power I need.»

When you pray this prayer sincerely, Jesus answers at once and justifies you before God and makes you His child.

Please write to me and I will pray for you and help you as you go on with Jesus Christ...

If you have received the Lord Jesus-Christ after reading this book, please write to us at the following addresse :

For Europe :

Editions du Livre Chrétien

4, Rue du Révérend Père Cloarec

92400 Courbevoie

Courriel : editionlivrechretien@gmail.com

TRUE CONVERSION (MARK 10:17-31)

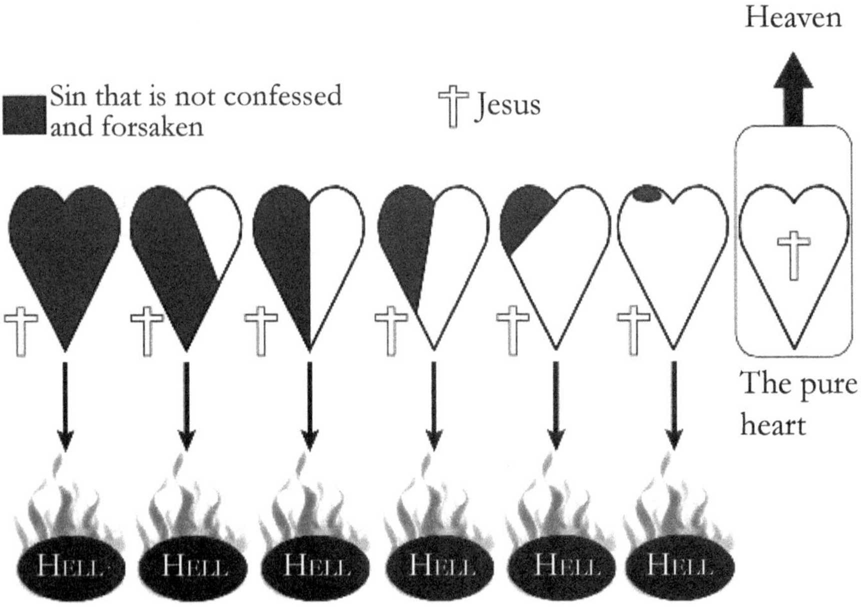

All the blemished hearts represent unsaved persons. The last pure heart alone represents the saved person.

Jesus cannot come in to blot out some of a person's sins and not others. He comes in to blot out all sins or no sin at all.

He blots out sin that is confessed and forsaken forever.

He comes in to be Saviour, Lord and King in all things and in all circumstances or He does not come in at all.

He cannot come in to be Saviour without being Lord and King because He cannot divide Himself. He is Saviour, Lord and King of all or Saviour, Lord and King of nothing at all.

Professor Zacharias Tanee Fomum

About the author

Professor Z.T. Fomum was born in 1945 in Cameroon and was taken to be with the Lord on the 14th March 2009. He was admitted to the Bachelor of Science degree, graduating as a prize-winning student from Fourah Bay College in the University of Sierra Leone. His research in Organic Chemistry earned him a Ph.D. degree in the University of Makerere, Kampala, Uganda. Recently, his published scientific work was evaluated and found to be of high distinction, earning him the award of a Doctor of Science degree from the University of Durham in Great Britain. As a Professor of Organic Chemistry in the University of Yaoundé I, Cameroon, he supervised and co-supervised more than 100 Master's and Doctoral degree theses. He published with others over 160 scientific articles in leading international journals.

The author read over 1350 books on the Christian Faith and wrote over 150 titles to advance the Gospel of Christ. 4 million copies of these books are in circulation in 11 languages, as well as 16 million gospel tracts in 17 languages. In pursuance of the purpose to proclaim the Gospel of Jesus Christ, he also made a total of over 700 missionary journeys in Cameroon and over 500 in 70 nations. These ranged from 2 days to 6 weeks in all the world's six continents.

The author led a Church-planting and missionary-sending movement, by whose ministrations, more than 10,000 healing miracles were performed by God in answer to prayer in the name of Jesus. These miracles include instant healings of; headaches, cancers, HIV/AIDS, blindness, deafness, dumbness, paralysis, madness and diverse diseases.

The author was married to Prisca Zei Fomum and they had 7 children who are all actively involved in serving the Lord. Prisca is a national and international minister specialising in the winning and discipling of children to Jesus Christ. She also communicates and imparts the vision of the ministry to children, with a view to raise and build up ministers for them.

The author owed all that he was and all that God had done in him and through him, to the unmerited favours and blessings of God and to his world wide army of friends and co-workers. He considered himself nothing without them and the blessings of God, and would have amounted to nothing but for them.

May the Lord receive all the glory!

Others books by Zacharias Tanee Fomum

- THE CHRISTIAN WAY
- The way of life
- The way of obedience
- The way of discipleship
- The way of sanctification
- The way of Christian character
- The way of spiritual power
- The way of Christian service
- The way of spiritual warfare
- The way of overcomers
- The way of suffering for Christ
- The way of spiritual encouragement
- The way of loving the Lord
- The way of victorious praying

-

- THE PRAYER
- The ministry of fasting
- The art of intercession
- The practice of intercession
- Praying with power
- Practical spiritual warfare through prayer
- Moving God through prayer
- The ministry of praise and thanksgiving
- Waiting on the Lord in prayer
- The ministry of supplication
- Life-changing thoughts on prayer, Vol 1
- Life-changing thoughts on prayer, Vol 2
- Life-changing thoughts on prayer, Vol 3
- The centrality of prayer

-

- PRACTICAL HELPS FOR OVERCOMERS
- The use of time
- Retreats for spiritual progress
- Personal spiritual revival
- Daily dynamic encounters with God
- The school of truth
- How to succeed in the Christian life
- The Christian and money
- Deliverance from the sin of laziness
- The art of working hard
- Knowing God – The greatest need of the hour
- Restitution : An important message for the overcomers
- Revelation a must
- True repentance
- You can receive a pure heart today
- You can lead someone to the Lord Jesus today
- The overcomer as a servant of man
- You have a talent!
- The Making of Disciples
- The secret of spiritual fruitfulness
- The dignity of manual labour

-

- GOD, SEX AND YOU
- Enjoying the premarital life
- Enjoying the choice of your marriage partner
- Enjoying the married life
- Divorce and remarriage
- A successful marriage; the husband's making
- A successful marriage; the wife's making

-

- EVANGELISATION
- God's love and forgiveness
- Come back home my son; I still love you
- Jesus loves you and wants to heal you
- Come and see; Jesus has not changed!
- 36 reasons for winning the lost to Christ
- Soul winning, Volume 1
- Soulwinning, Volume 2
- Celebrity a mask

-